...men's and general-interest
...s *Fitness*, *Slimming World* and other
with *Snoring and Sleep Apnoea*, *Coping with Childhood Asthma*,
with *Dyspraxia*, *Coping with Childhood Allergies*, *Helping Children Cope with Anxiety*, *Every Woman's Guide to Heart Health* and *Living with Eczema*, seven books written by Jill for Sheldon Press, were all published between 2003 and 2007. She lives beside the Regent's Canal in north London with two cats.

Overcoming Common Problems Series

Selected titles

A full list of titles is available from Sheldon Press,
36 Causton Street, London SW1P 4ST and on our website at
www.sheldonpress.co.uk

Overcoming Common Problems

Every Woman's Guide to Digestive Health

JILL ECKERSLEY

First published in Great Britain in 2008

Sheldon Press
36 Causton Street
London SW1P 4ST

Copyright © Jill Eckersley 2008

The author and publisher have made every effort to ensure that the
external website and email addresses included in this book are correct and
up to date at the time of going to press. The author and publisher are not
responsible for the content, quality or continuing accessibility of the sites.

British Library Cataloguing-in-Publication Data
A catalogue record for this book is available from the British Library

ISBN 978-1-84709-029-4

1 3 5 7 9 10 8 6 4 2

Typeset by Fakenham Photosetting Ltd, Fakenham, Norfolk
Printed in Great Britain by Ashford Colour Press

Produced on paper from sustainable forests

Contents

Acknowledgements

Writing this book would not have been possible without the help and co-operation of the many experts – doctors, patients and health professionals – who spared the time to talk to me.

Special thanks go to Dr John Bennett of CORE (the Digestive Disorders Foundation), Dr Suneil Kapadia, Professor Peter Molan, GP Dr Sarah Jarvis, acupuncturist Jessica Kennedy and dietitian Emma Mills.

I am also very grateful to the case study subjects who shared their stories with me.

Introduction

'A bad digestion is the root of all evil.' So said the Ancient Greek physician Hippocrates, the father of medicine, as long ago as 400 BC. Dr John Bennett, chairman of CORE (the Digestive Disorders Foundation), says that in the twenty-first century, the UK's digestive health is far from good. Gastrointestinal causes are responsible for 17 per cent of deaths, according to the Office of National Statistics, and Britain's doctors wrote out a whopping 60 million prescriptions for gastrointestinal disorders in 2002, costing the NHS (National Health Service) £802 million. Given that most of us don't take our sore stomachs to the doctor every time they cause us problems, preferring to dose ourselves with over-the-counter or home remedies, that adds up to an awful lot of stomach ache. In the year ending December 2006, consumers in England, Scotland and Wales bought 92.2 million packs of over-the-counter remedies for digestive ailments, worth £263.8 million. This includes 48.3 million packs of indigestion remedies, worth £126.4 million! And that doesn't count the money spent in health-food stores on complementary and 'alternative' remedies, or remedies bought by mail order.

Many digestive disorders are the so-called 'minor' ones like indigestion, heartburn, constipation, diarrhoea or food poisoning, the kind of thing that we accept as part of life but which, if they recur, can make us feel pretty miserable and below par. We don't just want to be 'not-ill'; we want to feel really well, and it's difficult to feel that if your stomach is out of order. 'Good health begins on the inside' is one of the slogans for CORE's Gut Week, a campaign which has been running annually for the past nine years.

There are some signs that minor digestive problems tend to affect women more than men. A 2005 survey for the *Reader's*

Digest and the Proprietary Association of Great Britain (PAGB), which represents the consumer healthcare industry, found that slightly more women than men reported problems with indigestion, upset stomachs and diarrhoea, and that far more women than men reported problems with constipation and IBS (irritable bowel syndrome).

Digestive disorders can also be serious, even fatal. Cancers of the digestive tract are actually the country's largest cancer killer, accounting for 23 per cent of all cancer deaths. Bowel cancer – the disease that killed World Cup hero Bobby Moore – is the second biggest cancer killer in the UK and the third most common cancer, affecting more than 35,000 people every year. Liver and pancreatic disease can also be killers and some of these illnesses are on the increase, mainly because of increased alcohol intake. Irritable bowel syndrome, which is not life threatening but can make life difficult for those living with it, is now estimated to affect between 10 and 22 per cent of the population.

Part of the problem with digestive disorders, according to CORE, is that it's not a subject we find easy to talk about. 'People will talk to you on social occasions about their heart attack, or even asthma, but not about their latest attack of diarrhoea and vomiting, or even belly ache. We are trying to correct this, but it's slow,' says Dr Bennett. The result is that many just accept poor digestive health as part of everyday life, and are not sure when – or even if – to go to the GP about that stomach ailment that just never seems to go away. Many of us know very little about how our digestive system works, or about the simple, everyday things we can do to make sure that we are looking after our stomachs and bowels in the same way that we look after our hearts, joints and the other systems in our bodies.

You can have a healthier digestion, one that enables you to enjoy your food without worrying whether something is going to upset you, or whether you will be able to go on an outing or take part in a special occasion like an examination or a family wedding without your insides playing up and spoiling the day. Sensible eating is one way to take care of your digestive system and we shall be looking at what that means in this book. We shall also be looking at the enemies of good digestion, including smoking, stress and excessive alcohol consumption as well as the rising tide of obesity, which is a major factor in the rise of indigestion-type complaints.

If you have picked up this book because you are keen to take responsibility for your own digestive health, and find out what you can do to stop things going wrong as well as how to cope when and if they ever do, then read on.

Note to the reader

This is not a medical book and is not intended to replace advice from your doctor. Consult your pharmacist or doctor if you believe you have any of the symptoms described, and if you think you might need medical help.

1

Digestive health: the facts

If you have problems with your digestion, you should at least be aware that you're not alone. Surveys of the British public's digestive health in 2006 showed that:

- one-third of the population regularly suffer from digestive illnesses such as irritable bowel syndrome (IBS), constipation, diarrhoea, stomach aches, nausea and sickness;
- six out of ten Britons say they have experienced digestive problems in stressful situations – including job interviews, moving house, divorce and exams;
- women, people in the South of England, and office or public-service workers such as nurses are most likely to experience stress-related gut disorders, and those who work outdoors are least likely;
- 31 per cent of people with a gut condition suffer at least once a week from it;
- 33 per cent of people with a gut condition think it is too trivial and not serious enough to bother the doctor with;
- some conditions, such as irritable bowel syndrome, are more common in women than men and about 10 per cent more women than men die from gastrointestinal disease;
- men get more alcohol-related gastrointestinal disease than women but women are beginning to catch up.

Christine, 53, has been living with her digestive problems ever since she was a teenager.

Any kind of acid fruit seemed to set off upper gastric pain, and I practically lived on Milk of Magnesia. I put up with it for years, thinking it was 'just one of those things' and taking everything I could find on the

1

chemists' shelves from Rennies to PeptoBismol. Nothing really seemed to help and what was worse, the problem spread to my bladder so I had recurrent cystitis too.

It was only about five years ago that I went to my GP saying that my poor digestion was ruining my life. I was given lots of tests including one for *Helicobacter pylori*, which came back negative. I was still put on antibiotics though, and they had no effect. Eventually I was sent for an endoscopy and they found 'inflammation and ulcerations of the duodenum'. I was prescribed ranitidine and then omeprazole, neither of which were very helpful.

Living with a digestion like mine can be really difficult. I would say I have to cancel about half of my work and social appointments because I don't feel well enough to go. I have even cancelled holidays at the last moment which hasn't made me very popular with my friends! Going out to dinner can be a problem because I always have to ask what any dish is made of, as I know I can't tolerate onions, peppers, garlic, acid fruits and lots of other things. I can never take chances with food or enjoy exotic meals and I have to restrict drinking alcohol to maybe one glass of red wine. Even then, I get a lot of stomach upsets.

I've tried the 'alternative' approach, giving up wheat and dairy for a while, but it didn't help. I've had three months of Chinese herbs and acupuncture which didn't work either. The only thing that helps at all is old-fashioned bicarbonate of soda. I take about half a flat teaspoonful in warm water. It tastes revolting but it does help. Apart from that it just seems to be something I have to live with.

Christine may be an extreme case, but there are many like her, struggling with recurrent digestive problems which seem to be triggered partly by diet and partly by stress. We'll be looking at dietary changes, and the effect of stress on the digestive system, in later chapters.

We've already seen in the Introduction how much the National Health Service spends on gastrointestinal disorders. Upper abdominal discomfort or dyspepsia, the sort of pain that Christine suffers, costs the NHS £500 million a year alone and accounts for 10 per cent of all drug costs in the NHS. Looked at another way, indigestion costs £11.25 per year for each of us.

There is some good news. The discovery, as recently as 1989, that the bacterium *Helicobacter pylori* is one of the chief causes of stomach and duodenal ulcers has led to the development of effective treatment with antibiotics and drugs such as the H2 blockers (like ranitidine) and proton-pump inhibitors (like omeprazole). In the past, patients with ulcers were prescribed a dull diet of milk and boiled fish, and ulcers often recurred. Earlier diagnosis and better treatment of digestive cancers are also more common, with the country's 'rolling programme' of screening for bowel cancers now up and running, and new drugs and drug combinations being used to treat cancer when it occurs. The charity Bowel Cancer UK estimates that by 2009 around 1,000 or 1,500 lives a year in England alone will be saved by the screening programme.

With the trend for most people to prefer to take control of their own lives and their own health, rather than waiting to be 'made better' by doctors, though, we have to start asking more questions about why our digestive health is so poor. Is there something we are doing (smoking? drinking too much alcohol? allowing ourselves to become obese?) or is there something about our diet (too many rich, fatty, or processed foods?) or the way we eat (on the run?) that is interfering with healthy, normal digestive processes?

Suneil Kapadia is a consultant in gastroenterology, based in Wolverhampton. He says that while there has been a large increase in some kinds of gut problem, others are less frequently encountered.

> For example, the incidence of oesophageal cancer – cancer of the gullet – has increased by a massive 50% in the last twenty years and bile duct tumours are also more common. The causes of this are unclear although they are being looked into. Both are conditions which are commoner in old age and smoking and alcohol could be a factor. I have also seen an explosion in the amount of fatty liver disease in recent years though I have no scientific evidence to prove it. Gastroenterologists like myself feel that people

are eating too much and exercising insufficiently, hence the rise in obesity which is not good news for gut health.

A phenomenal amount of money is spent on medicines for gut problems, both on prescription and over-the-counter, and GP consultations for gut problems cost the country something like £135 million a year. The trouble is that people tend to be embarrassed about having bowel problems and the subject gets brushed under the carpet.

Prevention of gut problems is also an area which doesn't get a lot of attention. Cardiologists have been good at getting the message across that the way to look after your heart is to eat less animal fat and exercise more, and there are also a lot of large-scale studies on the use of drugs like aspirin and statins to prevent heart disease. The National Health Service has a special framework for the prevention and treatment of some conditions, such as heart disease, diabetes and respiratory disease. GPs get points and extra money for taking preventative measures like checking blood pressure and cholesterol levels, but there is nothing like that for gastrointestinal disease.

Dr Kapadia points out that there have been some helpful initiatives, such as the introduction of screening for colo-rectal cancer in patients between the ages of 59 and 69, which was introduced in July 2006 in England. Scotland introduced a similar rolling programme of two-yearly checks in June 2007 and Wales and Northern Ireland are expected to follow suit. Those taking part are sent a testing kit and asked to send a stool sample to be analysed. If there is any cause for concern, people will be referred for further investigations or repeat tests. Over-70s can request a kit themselves by calling 0800 707 6060. As around 90 per cent of cases of colon cancer are diagnosed in the over-55 age group, and the incidence of this kind of cancer is increasing, it is hoped that screening will bring results. As with most cancers, the earlier it is diagnosed, the better the chances of recovery, though at present survival rates in Britain lag behind the rest of Europe.

'As far as prevention is concerned, there is no way to guarantee that you will have a healthy digestive system,' says Dr Kapadia.

As far as we know, it's not possible to prevent some cancers or inflammatory bowel diseases like Crohn's and colitis [see pp. 26–7 for more information on these conditions]. I advise my patients to do everything in moderation, eating a healthy balanced diet with plenty of roughage, and to get plenty of exercise. Many don't realize that alcohol affects the digestive system by damaging not only the liver but also the pancreas. For some people, heavy drinking is a part of life. They might be able to get away with it in their 20s and 30s, but by the time they are struggling, it's too late and the damage is already done.

Dr Kapadia also demolishes some of the myths surrounding stomach and bowel health, although he says there is some truth in some received wisdom! He says,

It is a good idea to eat a fibre-rich diet. A researcher in the 1930s and 1940s found that Africans get fewer digestive cancers and also less diverticular disease, probably because they have more roughage in their diet.

However, it isn't true that you necessarily have to have a bowel movement once a day. People do vary, and what's normal for you is what counts. The vast majority of healthy people 'go' anything from once or twice a day to two or three times a week, and anything between is 'normal'.

There is a lot of quackery out there. I come across people who are told they are 'allergic' to coffee or other drinks or foods, or told they have 'systemic candidiasis' – which is actually a very serious condition which affects the whole system and not something you can walk around with. There are more myths than scientific observations – for instance there is no science to the fashionable 'colonic irrigation'. The body just doesn't build up toxins which need to be removed in that way. You may feel better after a detox, so-called, but the body is very stable and nothing will really have altered.

It's the same with drinking litres and litres of water which I have seen recommended. Obviously if you don't get enough fluids it can aggravate constipation if you are prone to it, but there is no ideal amount, it depends on your size and build.

2

Know your digestion

Your digestive system – or gut, or alimentary tract – is basically a tube, some nine metres long, which extends all the way from your mouth to your bowel. Its job is to take in and then process every scrap of food that you eat, so that all the nutrients, vitamins and minerals on which your health depends are extracted from it, absorbed into your bloodstream and sent on their way to build up every cell in your body. What's left, the waste matter, is then passed out of the body as faeces.

Each part of the system has its own job to do. The mouth produces saliva, containing enzymes which begin to break down the food into smaller particles which can be used by the body. Once chewed up and swallowed, food passes down the gullet or oesophagus which is the link between the mouth and the stomach. Muscles in the gullet contract in rhythmic waves to push the food down. These contractions are so powerful that you could actually eat and swallow food standing on your head! Chewing and swallowing are among the very few digestive actions which are under your conscious control. Once your food has been swallowed, your digestive system deals with it automatically.

Your stomach is a J-shaped bag, situated in the upper part of your abdomen, between your lower ribs and your navel. An adult stomach can hold about one and a half litres of food or liquid at a time. Food remains in the stomach for about four hours, during which time it is mixed with gastric juices, including enzymes which help to break down the food still further, and acid. The enzyme pepsin, found in the stomach, converts the proteins in food into substances called peptides, and eventually into individual amino acids, which can be absorbed in the small intestine.

Stomach acid is extremely strong. Its job is to kill most of the bacteria and it is similar to the acids used to clean metal – indeed, a coin retrieved from the stomach of a toddler was found to have holes in it made by stomach acids! However, the acid doesn't damage the stomach itself as the walls are protected by a thick layer of mucus. The cells in this lining are renewed every three days or so for complete protection.

Food then passes via the duodenum – a short tube – to the small intestine. This part of the digestive system is approximately six and a half metres long and has a vast surface area. Rather than being completely smooth, it is covered with very small folds, called villi and micro-villi, through which the goodness in the food, now reduced to tiny particles, can be absorbed into the bloodstream. It has been estimated that, if the surface of the small intestine could be stretched out flat, it would be the size of a tennis court. Like the stomach, the small intestine has a protective lining of mucus.

From the small intestine, what is left of the food is passed to the large intestine or colon, where any remaining nutrients are processed and absorbed in their turn. Food remnants can remain in the large intestine for anything from twelve to 48 hours, depending on the type of food. The large intestine also contains most of what are known as your 'intestinal flora' or bacteria. 400 to 500 different species of bacteria, such as lactobacillus and bifidobacteria, reside in the colon, mostly in the mucous membrane which forms the lining. These are usually described as 'good' or 'friendly' bacteria and there are an unbelievable thousand billion of them in a healthy colon. Their function is to break down most of the remaining undigested material in the food. Water and mineral salts also pass through the lining of the large intestine into the bloodstream. Good bacteria also help the digestive system to remain healthy by stimulating the movement of the gut, so that food passes through it at the right rate, by discouraging the growth of bacteria which could be harmful, such as *E. coli* and *Staphylococcus aureus*, and by breaking down the undigested particles of food. They also help to produce vitamin K, which is used by the body to help in the clotting of blood.

Food residue, liquids and undigested matter pass along the digestive tract by the same rhythmic waves – called peristalsis – to the rectum. When the bowel is full, the body receives a signal that it is time to empty it by passing faeces.

Other organs are also important in the digestive process. Among them are the salivary glands in the mouth, the liver, pancreas and gall bladder. The salivary glands produce enzymes which begin the breakdown of carbohydrates in our food into simpler substances which the body can absorb. The enzyme amylase turns starch into maltose, and then the enzyme maltase turns that into glucose. The enzyme sucrase turns sucrose into glucose, and the enzyme lactase turns lactose into glucose.

The liver is the largest gland in the body. Women's livers weigh about 1.3 kg on average, compared to men's livers which weigh 1.8 kg. The liver is situated below the ribs on the right-hand side of the body. It is capable of holding about a pint of blood at any one time, and has more than 500 functions, many of which are involved in digestion. For example, the liver produces about one pint of bile every day. This is stored in the gall bladder and then flows through the bile duct into the small intestine to help with digestion. The liver also

- produces quick energy. We have already seen that enzymes in saliva break down carbohydrates into glucose, which is stored in the liver and muscles as glycogen. The liver then converts its store of glycogen back into glucose, ready to be used;
- helps to process digested food and absorb nutrients;

- controls the levels of fats, amino acids and glucose in the blood;
- neutralizes and destroys toxins;
- helps to clean the blood;
- stores some vitamins, iron and other essential chemicals;
- helps the body to get rid of waste.

The pancreas, a small organ about 15 cm long, situated deep within the body in the upper abdomen, produces enzymes which turn some of the elements in food – fats, carbohydrates and proteins – into simpler substances that the body can absorb. The enzyme lipase, for example, found in the pancreas and small intestine, helps to turn lipids (fats and oils) from food into fatty acids and glycerol. It also secretes hormones which affect the levels of sugar in the blood, and produces chemicals which neutralize stomach acid.

The gall bladder is a small pear-shaped organ about 9 cm long which stores bile, a greenish-yellow liquid produced by the liver and delivered into the digestive system during a meal to help emulsify fats so that both fats and certain vitamins – A, D, E and K – can be more easily absorbed into the bloodstream.

3

What can go wrong?

As we have already seen, the alimentary canal is a complex collection of organs, each with several separate but related functions, so it's not surprising that things can go wrong. In this chapter we shall be looking at everyday gastric problems – what they are, what causes them, how they can be avoided if possible and how they are best treated.

Indigestion, or dyspepsia to give it its other common name, is something we're all familiar with. It is the feeling of discomfort or actual pain in the upper part of the abdomen or the chest which often affects us after eating. Some people experience frequent indigestion and their symptoms may include, as well as pain, an over-full or bloated feeling, heaviness, burping, a rumbling stomach and nausea (feeling sick). The symptoms may last for just a short time or for hours. While not usually a sign that there's anything seriously wrong, indigestion is uncomfortable and unpleasant especially if it occurs after every meal.

If you are prone to indigestion you can often help yourself by taking these common-sense precautions:

- Eat small regular meals and avoid fatty and spicy foods, as well as any food items which you know are liable to upset you.
- Eat slowly and chew your food carefully, making sure you don't gulp down too much air with your meals. Try to keep mealtimes calm and relaxed occasions rather than bolting your food with one eye on the clock.
- Give up smoking (we shall be looking at the effect smoking has on digestive health in Chapter 6).

- Avoid late-night meals. Allow time for your food to be digested properly before going to bed.
- Avoid too much coffee and alcohol, especially late at night.
- Make sure that any medications you are taking, for instance painkillers and anti-arthritis drugs, are not causing your digestive problems. If your medication disagrees with you, ask your GP or specialist if there is an alternative.

Heartburn and hiatus hernia

Heartburn is a particular type of indigestion which causes a burning sensation behind the breastbone, which may feel as if it is spreading upwards from the stomach towards the throat. Some people even regurgitate acid or have a strong 'acidic' feeling in the throat or chest. It can be unpleasant but again, is not usually harmful.

We have already seen in Chapter 2 that the stomach produces very strong acid which is used in the early stages of the digestive process. Normally, this acid is kept in the stomach by a muscle which acts like a valve, in the upper chest where the oesophagus or gullet joins the stomach. Occasionally, however, some of this acid is able to leak out into the gullet. It can irritate and damage the delicate lining and, not surprisingly, causes pain. 'Acid reflux' is another name for this condition. If symptoms are especially severe and persistent, it is referred to as GORD, or gastro-oesophageal reflux disease.

People who smoke, drink a lot of alcohol, are under stress or are overweight are especially prone to heartburn, as are mothers-to-be. During pregnancy, hormonal changes may relax the muscle at the top of the stomach which normally prevents acid reflux and the growing baby in the womb may lead to pressure on the stomach. Some people's stomachs actually produce too much acid, but the main cause of heartburn is acid in the wrong place – which means in the oesophagus rather than in the stomach.

Another condition which can cause heartburn is hiatus hernia. The diaphragm is a sheet of muscle which separates the chest and lungs from the abdomen. Its weakest point is known as the hiatus, and is where the oesophagus or gullet joins the stomach. Occasionally part of the stomach can slip through at this point and this is called a hiatus hernia. Again, stomach acid can cause pain although some people with a hiatus hernia do not have any symptoms. The over-50s, pregnant women, the overweight and smokers are most at risk of hiatus hernia, which can be treated with medication or, in a few cases, surgery.

'My hiatus hernia causes heartburn and reflux problems and definitely gets worse when I'm under stress,' says Lynn, 39.

> I haven't found any really effective medication. My GP suggested eating my main meal at lunch-time and not eating after six at night, which really does seem to help. If I am forced to eat later, I try not to go to bed until my stomach is empty, even if I have to prop my eyes open!
>
> It does have an impact on my social life. I feel like a wet blanket at dinner parties when everyone else is munching away and knocking back the wine. I am now considering keyhole surgery to repair the hernia.

The precautions recommended for avoiding indigestion can also help you to avoid heartburn. Trigger foods, as well as the obvious ones like very spicy curries or very fatty foods, can include anything from chocolate, cucumber and onions to citrus fruits. If you get a lot of heartburn, you should make a note of what you have recently eaten so that you can learn to avoid your personal trigger foods.

Some medicines can also worsen heartburn symptoms in susceptible people. These can include nitrates, prescribed for heart conditions, calcium channel blockers, prescribed for angina, and some antibiotics. If you think this might be your problem ask your GP if there are alternatives you can use.

Lifestyle changes such as giving up smoking and losing any excess weight can also help. Even something as simple as avoiding very tight clothing, or sitting down quietly after a meal rather than leaping up to do something can also reduce the symptoms. Don't exercise straight after a heavy meal. If you find that your heartburn is worse at night, try sleeping on extra pillows or raising the head of your bed on wooden blocks, so that gravity will keep the acid down in your stomach where it belongs.

Both indigestion and heartburn are usually treated with over-the-counter medicines which can be very effective. They include antacids – often aluminium compounds, magnesium compounds, calcium compounds or sodium bicarbonate – which, as their name suggests, neutralize any excess acid produced by your stomach. Brand names to look out for include Bisodol. Alginates lie on top of your stomach to prevent any of the acid contents escaping into your oesophagus and causing pain. Brand names include Gaviscon. Acid reducers actually stop your stomach from producing excess acid. Brand names include Zantac and PepcidTwo.

If trapped wind is the problem, and you suffer from griping pains which you know would be relieved by releasing it, you can buy anti-flatulents like Rennie Deflatine and Wind-Eze. They contain compounds which will make it easier for you to burp or pass wind. Some people feel uncomfortable after eating simply because their stomachs don't seem to work very effectively and it takes longer than average for food to be 'processed' and passed into the small intestine, the next stage on its journey through the alimentary canal. If this is your problem, you can feel full or bloated even when you haven't eaten very much. You might feel heavy and nauseous and generally uncomfortable rather than experiencing real pain. These symptoms might be best treated by a motility restorer such as domperidone (Motilium 10) which you can buy at a pharmacy, or metoclopromide (Maxolon) which your GP can prescribe. These drugs will help the digestive processes to start moving normally again.

Some of the products you can buy contain combinations of these ingredients. Rennie Duo, for example, contains both antacids and sodium alginate, as do Gaviscon Double Action and Setlers Liquid. If you need advice on which of the many brands would be best for you, ask your pharmacist, giving as many details of your symptoms as possible. It is also important to read the information on the pack as well as the instruction leaflet to make sure that the product you have chosen is appropriate. Pregnant women should be especially careful to ensure that anything they take is suitable.

Constipation

In our grandmothers' day, people were expected to go to the toilet once a day without fail, and anyone who didn't have a regular-as-clockwork bowel movement would be 'dosed' with something like syrup of figs. Today more is known about the workings of the normal, healthy bowel and it's important to realize that you don't have to go every day. What is important is what's normal for you, and in this country that can mean anything from three bowel movements a day to three a week. As long as your bowel movements are solid, but soft and easy to pass without a lot of straining, there's no need to worry about constipation.

'Once a day is not a rule,' says consultant gastroenterologist Suneil Kapadia.

> Bowel habits do vary but the majority of people in this country go from once or twice a day to two or three times a week. Sometimes there is a genuine reason why you don't go often – for example, an under-active thyroid can make you constipated, as can some forms of medication – or it could be just the way you are.

You are constipated if you don't open your bowels more than twice a week, you have to strain to pass a stool, or you produce dry, hard stools like rabbit droppings. You might have other symptoms too, like headaches or a general feeling of unwellness or discomfort. Too much straining can also lead to piles. Constipation isn't actually harmful, unless it's very severe. There is a lot you can do to help your sluggish bowel to do its job properly without resorting to laxatives. For instance:

- Make sure you get plenty of fibre (roughage) in your diet. This doesn't mean overdosing on bran, though a bran cereal in the morning can sometimes help. The 'five-a-day' rule for fruit and vegetables should be an absolute minimum. Eat wholemeal bread and pasta, have salad in your sandwiches at lunchtime and/or a side salad with your evening meal, and at least two portions of vegetables with main meals. Snack on fruit, either fresh or dried, and preferably unpeeled. Some people find that starting the day with a glass of warm water and a slice of lemon helps.

- Ensure you develop and maintain healthy bowel habits. If at all possible, don't ignore the urge to go to the lavatory. This often happens naturally first thing in the morning or after a meal. If you don't go when your body needs to, the stool may dry up and become harder and more difficult to pass next time. Allow yourself time, even on busy workday mornings, to go to the lavatory, until it becomes routine.

- Drink plenty of water. Constipation is sometimes the result of general dehydration. Your morning coffee can sometimes start your bowels working by itself. Make a habit of keeping a glass or bottle of water on your desk at work, or having a drink each time you pass the kitchen sink. You don't have to drink gallons of water, but lack of fluid in your system can certainly aggravate constipation if you are prone to it.

- Exercise can also help to relieve constipation, so get moving. Try to incorporate more exercise into your everyday life by walking to work, taking the children to school on foot, shopping locally rather than taking the car to the supermarket, going for a family walk at the weekend instead of slumping in front of the TV. Gardening, housework and DIY can also be pretty strenuous and help to get your insides working.

If changing your diet, drinking more liquid and exercising more don't seem to have any effect on your constipation, you might consider the short-term use of laxatives, many of which are available without a doctor's prescription. As an occasional or temporary measure, this can be helpful, but it's wise not to depend on laxative use to keep you 'regular'.

Basically there are three different kinds of laxatives, which are available in different forms – tablets, chewable tablets, even drinks. Stimulant laxatives just speed up bowel movement, and usually work within 8 to 12 hours, so that if you take them at night you should be able to have a bowel movement next morning. Examples include the traditional senna (contained in Ex-Lax and Senokot) and syrup of figs, and also bisacodyl (Dulcolax) and docusate sodium (DulcoEase).

Bulk-forming laxatives, as their name suggests, swell up inside the bowel to increase the amount of stool and encourage bowel movement. This is how bran works. Many OTC (over-the-counter) laxatives such as Fybogel contain ispaghula husk and some are available in the form of fruit-flavoured drinks. It's especially important to drink plenty of liquid when you take this type of laxative.

Osmotic laxatives draw more water into the bowel, making stools softer and therefore easier to pass. Magnesium salts like Andrews and Epsom salts work in this way as do lactulose syrup, Movicol and Idrolax, phosphate enemas and sodium citrate.

As with all OTC medicines, it's important that you read the instructions carefully before taking any laxatives as an over-dose can cause uncomfortable wind, stomach cramps and even diarrhoea.

Diarrhoea

Like constipation and indigestion, diarrhoea is something which affects almost everyone at some point in their lives. It means the passing of frequent, watery stools, often accompanied by griping pains in the stomach. This happens when something – possibly a virus or bacterium – irritates the lining of the small or large intestine, causing it to contract strongly. Too much fluid is passed from the bloodstream into the bowel, or the bowel moves its contents onwards more swiftly than usual. Acute diarrhoea, lasting just a few hours or days, may be caused by infected food (food poisoning), gastroenteritis (see p. 18), a change of diet (holiday tummy), excessive alcohol consumption, or extreme anxiety, as in exam nerves or stage fright.

Chronic diarrhoea – lasting longer than just a few days – may be caused by a functional condition such as irritable bowel syndrome, inflammation of the bowel in conditions like ulcerative colitis or Crohn's disease, or a condition where food is poorly absorbed such as coeliac disease (gluten intolerance). Food intolerance can also lead to diarrhoea, although true food allergies tend to be rarer than people think! Some kinds of medication, including commonly prescribed ones like antibiotics, can also cause diarrhoea in susceptible people. We shall be looking at these conditions in more detail later.

Acute diarrhoea usually cures itself within a few days. It can be treated with over-the-counter medicines such as loperamide (Imodium, Arret) or simply by restricting yourself to a bland diet of plain boiled rice or dry toast and plenty of water to drink, as severe diarrhoea can lead to dehydration.

It is often possible to prevent attacks of diarrhoea by taking sensible food hygiene precautions (see Chapter 4) and being careful what and where you eat when travelling abroad. Always wash your hands before preparing food and after using the toilet, playing with pets or working in the garden. It is better not to prepare food for other people, especially babies, toddlers and the elderly, while you are suffering from diarrhoea. If your job involves food serving or preparation, you are advised to wait 48 hours after your symptoms subside before going back to work.

Diarrhoea is not often serious but you should consult your doctor if

- it affects a baby or child under two;
- it affects an elderly person;
- the condition does not respond to home remedies such as those mentioned above;
- there is blood in the stools.

Gastroenteritis

Diarrhoea can be accompanied by vomiting, which is the body's way of ridding itself of any harmful or poisonous substance. Gastroenteritis is a very common and highly infectious condition leading to inflammation of the stomach and gut, usually caused by bacteria such as *E. coli*, salmonella or campylobacter, or viruses such as the Norwalk virus, rotaviruses and hepatitis A. Gastroenteritis may also produce a fever and stomach cramps, but is not usually serious. Careful attention to food hygiene and sensible precautions regarding hand-washing and disinfection of the home can help to stop the bug spreading.

Morning sickness

Vomiting is also common in early pregnancy. The causes are not known although it probably has something to do with hormonal changes in the body at this time. It's known as morning sickness although some unlucky women find that they feel nauseous for most of the day. In most cases it clears up after the first trimester, but if it doesn't or if it is very severe and you can't keep anything down, not even plain liquids, ask your doctor's advice as there is a risk of dehydration.

All pregnancy-related books and websites offer advice on coping with morning sickness. Tips include getting out of bed slowly and nibbling a dry biscuit first. Try to eat little and often, sticking to plain, easily digested foods. Drink plenty of liquids like water and fruit juice, avoiding tea and coffee. Ginger is a traditional remedy and can be taken as a tea, in ginger ale or as ginger biscuits.

Many pregnant women experiencing morning sickness are afraid their growing baby will not receive any nourishment. It's reassuring to know that babies in the womb are very good at obtaining the nourishment they need, however little the mother manages to eat!

Travel sickness

Travel sickness affects a lot of children, especially those between about three and 12, and some adults too. It isn't strictly speaking a digestive problem, but is caused by the motion of moving vehicles upsetting the balance mechanism in the inner ear. Sitting near the front of the car or coach, avoiding reading while travelling, eating light meals or nothing at all, getting plenty of fresh air and stopping regularly to stretch the legs, can all help. There are also many over-the-counter medicines including herbal and homeopathic preparations, which can be effective, for this nuisance condition.

Gastritis and ulcers

As explained in Chapter 2, the stomach produces very strong acid to help in the digestion of food, but is lined by a thick layer of mucus which prevents the acid from damaging the organ itself. Sometimes, though, the lining becomes inflamed, sore and irritated, which can cause considerable pain or gastritis. This kind of pain can come on suddenly and only last for a short time, or it can become a chronic condition.

Gastritis can be caused by excess alcohol consumption, infection with the bacterium *Helicobacter pylori* (which is also implicated in stomach and duodenal ulcers), the use of medication like aspirin and non-steroidal anti-inflammatories such as ibuprofen, and stress and anxiety which can cause the stomach to produce more acid than normal.

The lining of the stomach or duodenum may then develop a raw patch, rather like a mouth ulcer, which becomes extremely painful when it comes into contact with normal strong stomach acid. An ulcer may develop anywhere in the duodenum or stomach. In the 1980s, researchers discovered for the first time that most patients with stomach or duodenal ulcers have the bacterium *Helicobacter pylori* in the lining of their stomachs. About half the adults in the country carry this bacterium. It does not always lead to ulcers, and at present it is not known why only some carriers are affected.

Ulcers are very common – about one in 15 women will be affected during their lifetimes. They are likely to run in families and are more common in older people. Anxiety and stress are not thought to cause ulcers in themselves, contrary to popular belief, but they can make the symptoms – a burning pain behind the breastbone, heartburn, wind, nausea and sometimes vomiting – much worse. Neglected and untreated ulcers can lead to extreme pain and vomiting, including vomiting blood, a sign of internal bleeding. A 'perforated ulcer' counts as a medical emergency.

Gastritis and ulcers can now be treated with medication which is often extremely effective, although they can recur especially if you are not willing to adapt your lifestyle by, for example giving up smoking, cutting down on alcohol, and learning to relax more. Antacids (see p. 13) are often prescribed at first as they neutralize the stomach acid. More sophisticated drugs include the H2 receptor antagonists like ranitidine (Zantac) and cimetidine (Tagamet) which act by reducing the amount of stomach acid produced. More modern treatments than these include drugs called proton-pump inhibitors, such as lansoprazole (Zoton) and omeprazole (Losec) which can reduce the amount of stomach acid produced by as much as 70 per cent, giving the ulcerations time to heal.

Ulcers caused by *H. pylori* are now often treated by a week-long drug regime which combines acid-reducing drugs with antibiotics, and this can be very effective.

Some people still suffer from ulcer-type, upper gastric pain even though no ulcer is present. In this case, the diagnosis is usually non-ulcer dyspepsia, the causes of which are unknown. However the treatments and lifestyle changes recommended for ulcer patients may prove beneficial.

Irritable bowel syndrome (IBS)

IBS is one of the most common digestive disorders in the Western world. It affects about a third of the population of Britain at some time in their lives and it's estimated that more than half of all gastroenterology outpatients have IBS. It is sometimes described as a 'functional bowel disorder' because it affects the way the large intestine, or colon, actually works. As described in Chapter 2, the colon is a muscular tube which propels the contents of the alimentary tract along in a series of regular muscular contractions. In people with IBS, what should be a smooth painless process leads to painful muscle spasms. The 'irritable' bowel either works too slowly, or too quickly, leading to constipation or diarrhoea.

Symptoms of IBS vary from person to person but can include:

- abdominal pain, often colicky, and tenderness;
- bloating and a feeling of fullness;

- variation in bowel habit – some people get constipation, others diarrhoea, others both at different times;
- other varied symptoms like lethargy, back pain and painful periods.

As yet, the medical profession doesn't really know what causes IBS. All that can be said is that people with IBS have a more sensitive than average bowel, although there is no inflammation as there is in other conditions like colitis and Crohn's disease. Food intolerance may play a part. Some people say that their first bout of IBS-type symptoms followed an attack of gastroenteritis or an episode of food poisoning. Stress seems to play a part, with many people reporting that their condition worsens if they are upset. Living with a 'difficult' digestion and the embarrassment of having to rush to the toilet from time to time is, of course, stressful in itself and can make symptoms worse.

Many people with IBS-type symptoms are also concerned that they might be signs of more serious disease. It's important to realize, once you have a diagnosis of IBS, that it is not linked to cancer or any other serious condition. Neither is it 'all in the mind'. There is no cure as yet, although some of the symptoms, such as constipation or diarrhoea, can be treated with medication as and when they appear. Anti-spasmodic drugs such as mebeverine (Colofac) can also be prescribed for the cramping pains. Occasionally, tricyclic antidepressants such as amitryptiline, which can have a constipating effect, may also be prescribed.

Living with IBS may mean adapting your lifestyle to avoid any factors which make your symptoms worse. Unfortunately the only way of doing this is by trial and error. If constipation is one of your chief symptoms, you might benefit from a high-fibre diet, with plenty of fruit and vegetables and wholemeal bread. Confusingly, other people with IBS might actually be advised to eat less fibre. It is a very individual condition. Avoiding rich, fatty and/or spicy food may help, and better diet awareness may enable you to work out which, if any, foods trigger your digestive symptoms.

Actually receiving the diagnosis and understanding that, although unpleasant and sometimes embarrassing, IBS is not a life-threatening condition, can often help people to manage it better. Therapies which encourage relaxation, like yoga, meditation and Autogenic Training (see Chapter 7) may also be beneficial.

The campaigning charity, The Gut Trust (formerly the IBS Network; contact details on p. 115) offers help and support to anyone with IBS, their families and carers, and has up-to-date information on the latest research and treatments.

Haemorrhoids

Haemorrhoids, or 'piles' are really enlarged and swollen blood vessels in and around the lower rectum and anus. Around half of the population gets them at some time. They are caused by pressure on these blood vessels, and are often a side effect of constipation as straining causes the blood vessels to swell. Symptoms include discomfort, pain and soreness as well as itching and sometimes bleeding. Haemorrhoids can be internal or external and are especially common in pregnancy, as the weight of the baby in the womb presses on the vulnerable blood vessels in the lower part of the alimentary tract.

They often heal up by themselves, but if they are a continuous problem, ask your pharmacist about the over-the-counter creams available to treat them, which include Anusol, Germoloids and Preparation H. Most contain soothing ingredients such as zinc oxide plus lidocaine to help numb the area while the haemorrhoids heal. They are intended for short-term use, five to seven days at most. If symptoms persist, you are advised to consult your GP who may prescribe steroid ointments, or refer you to a specialist for an outpatient treatment called 'banding'. This involves placing a rubber band around the haemorrhoids, cutting off their blood supply so that they dry up. Surgery under a general anaesthetic is also a possibility.

Preventing piles from developing, or recurring, is largely a matter of avoiding constipation (see advice above) by making sure that you eat five or more portions of fruit and vegetables a day, drink plenty of fluids and exercise regularly.

You will see from the information in this chapter that digestive disorders are

- extremely common;
- painful, uncomfortable and a nuisance;
- often accompanied by the same symptoms of pain and disturbance of bowel function.

It isn't easy to tell whether particular symptoms are caused by something minor or something more serious. In the next chapter we shall be looking at more serious gastrointestinal problems and the need to check out your symptoms with your GP.

4

Could it be serious?

We have already seen that most digestive disturbances are extremely common and right themselves after a few days, whether or not you treat them with home remedies and over-the-counter medicines or just let them take their course. The symptoms of gastrointestinal illness are, unfortunately, difficult to differentiate from each other. Pain in your 'middle', bloating, wind, nausea, sickness, a change in your bowel habit – could all be symptoms of many disorders. Most of them are minor and easily cured. However, all the organizations and charities campaigning on behalf of gastrointestinal disease say that if you do have a more serious condition, early diagnosis is vital.

Always remember that the chances are that your stomach ache is far more likely to be the result of something like a dodgy burger, or of eating on-the-run, than it is of something more serious. However, if your symptoms seem to be recurring, or don't clear up with the help of over-the-counter remedies, it could be a sign that you should visit your GP just to check that there isn't anything seriously wrong.

CORE (the Digestive Disorders Foundation), and the British Society of Gastroenterology, have formulated a list of symptoms which you should look out for. One episode of unexplained stomach pain or diarrhoea is unlikely to be anything to worry about, but persistent gastric problems, for which there seems to be no apparent reason, should always be checked out. If you regularly experience

- abdominal pain before or after meals;
- feelings of fullness, bloating or flatulence;

- nausea or vomiting;
- heartburn or regurgitation;
- pain or difficulty in swallowing;
- loss of appetite;
- continuing and unexplained weight loss;
- indigestion;
- constipation, diarrhoea or any change in bowel habit which is unusual for you;
- changes in the appearance of your bowel motions, especially if they look black, dark red, very pale or contain mucus;
- pain or bleeding when you have a bowel movement (remembering that piles or haemorrhoids are by far the most common cause of bleeding from the bottom);
- feeling that your bowels are not emptying completely;
- any abdominal symptoms that make you feel tired, lethargic or unwell
- then make an appointment to see your doctor. The chances are that there is nothing seriously wrong but it's as well to be sure. If you do turn out to have a more serious gastrointestinal problem, early diagnosis and treatment can only help.

Digestive disorders can be divided into the chronic – conditions like colitis, Crohn's disease and coeliac disease, which can be treated with a combination of drugs, dietary changes and sometimes surgery – and acute conditions like appendicitis and gallstones, for which surgery is the most usual treatment. Cancers can also affect the digestive tract, as they can other parts of the body.

Inflammatory bowel disease

The two most common types of inflammatory bowel disease are Crohn's disease and ulcerative colitis, which, together, affect something like one in 400 people in the UK. Men and women are equally affected. As yet, the causes are unknown, although research is ongoing and in June 2007, the medical research charity the Wellcome Trust announced the discovery of three new genes for Crohn's disease, one of which links it to Type 1 diabetes.

There are other types of bowel inflammation (or colitis) which can cause similar symptoms, which may be intermittent and flare up at intervals. Ulcerative colitis leads to small ulcers developing on the lining of the colon, or large intestine. Crohn's disease, which was first recognized in the 1930s, leads to inflammation, scarring and ulceration of the walls of the small intestine and/or the colon – though the ulcers can affect any part of the digestive tract. It is sometimes difficult to distinguish between the two conditions since both can cause similar symptoms – abdominal pain, urgent diarrhoea which is sometimes bloodstained, excessive tiredness and loss of weight. Both can also be associated with other inflammatory conditions affecting the joints, eyes and skin.

There seems to be a genetic element involved in these conditions. People with relatives who have them seem to be at higher risk. Environmental factors are also involved – smoking makes Crohn's worse – but, as yet, no one has identified the causes.

Both Crohn's and ulcerative colitis are usually treated with drugs, with surgery as an option in serious cases and when drug treatments are not effective. Many people find that particular foods aggravate their symptoms or cause flare-ups, so a change in diet can sometimes help, as can stress-reduction techniques. Drugs which may be prescribed include steroids, which can reduce the inflammation, and immunosuppressants, which can prevent relapses. Another class of drugs, called aminosalicylates, is also used for anti-inflammatory effect. Most recently a new range of drugs called monoclonal antibodies has been introduced.

The National Association for Colitis and Crohn's Disease can offer a lot of helpful tips and support to those who have these and related conditions. Contact details are on p. 115.

Coeliac disease

Coeliac (pronounced see-liac) disease is another digestive condition which can produce a range of unpleasant symptoms, from bloating, diarrhoea/constipation, nausea, tiredness and anaemia to depression, infertility and joint pain. It is often thought of as a kind of allergy, because coeliacs are unable to digest gluten, a protein which is found in wheat, rye and barley (and is therefore present in a huge variety of everyday foodstuffs). Strictly speaking, however, coeliac disease is not an allergy but an autoimmune disease, in which the body produces antibodies which attack its own tissues.

Coeliac disease is a lifelong condition for which there is no cure at present. It can be managed by switching to a gluten-free diet, which is much easier now than it was in the past. Almost every major supermarket sells gluten-free products and specialist manufacturers make ranges of bread, cakes and other items which can be indistinguishable from 'the real thing'. Also, of course, there are many food items, for example meat, fish, vegetables and fruit, which don't contain gluten anyway so you don't have to live on a restricted diet.

In affected people, gluten damages the lining of the gut and the nutrients from food are not properly absorbed. There can be a higher-than-normal risk, for women, of developing the brittle bone condition osteoporosis because calcium from the diet hasn't been absorbed.

Because the symptoms of coeliac disease are easily confused with those of other conditions, many people carry on for years without a proper diagnosis. A simple blood test from your GP will reveal the antibodies typical of coeliac disease and you should then take advice from a dietitian or Coeliac UK, the campaigning and support group (contact details on p. 115), about your gluten-free diet regime. Once gluten is removed from the diet, some people feel better very quickly, although it can take months or years before full health is restored. About 1 in 100 Europeans has coeliac disease, which was first described in medical journals as long ago as the second century AD, although the link with gluten was not established until the 1940s.

Appendicitis

Conditions whose names end in '-itis' mean 'inflammation of...'. We have already seen that ulcerative colitis is inflammation of the colon, and appendicitis – the most common reason for emergency surgery in the UK – is inflammation of the appendix, a part of the human bowel which has always been thought to have no real purpose, since the human body appears to function perfectly well without it! However, in 2007 researchers at Duke University Medical School in North Carolina, USA, suggested that the original purpose of the appendix may have been to act as a kind of 'nursery' for good gut bacteria, releasing them when necessary into the intestines.

The appendix is a small tube-like organ, between 5 and 10 cm long, which is situated near the start of the colon or large bowel. Sometimes this organ becomes inflamed for no apparent reason. If it does it is usually removed in a routine surgical operation.

An inflamed appendix causes pain, usually starting in the centre of the abdomen and then often moving over to the lower right-hand side. The pain gradually gets worse and there many be nausea and even vomiting. The sore area becomes extremely tender and any pressure on it is very painful.

An inflamed appendix should be removed as if it bursts the infection can spread through the rest of the abdomen causing peritonitis, which is inflammation of the inner lining or peritoneum. This is a much more serious condition usually treated with antibiotics.

Gallstones

Gallstones can also cause severe abdominal pain, usually felt in the right upper abdomen, especially after a rich or fatty meal. The pain is usually situated below the ribs but may also be felt in the back or shoulder, and may be accompanied by fever and/ or nausea and sickness.

As explained in Chapter 2, the gall bladder is where bile, a liquid produced by the liver and used by the body to help digest fats, is stored. It then passes to the small intestine through the bile duct. Gallstones are hard pieces of material, ranging from tiny gravel-sized pieces to stones the size of a pea or even larger. They are made of cholesterol, plus chalk, and are more common in women than men. Many people have gallstones without experiencing any symptoms. However, if they lead to inflammation of the gall bladder, block the bile ducts, or pass into the duodenum, they can cause severe pain.

Those at risk include people with high cholesterol, perhaps because of a diet containing too much fat or too many refined carbohydrates. Age is a factor. About one in ten older people has gallstones.

Gallstones are sometimes discovered when other gastrointestinal investigations are taking place but are usually only treated when they cause pain. There are drugs which can dissolve them, or they can be treated with ultrasonic shock waves or removed by keyhole surgery.

Diverticulitis

As many as a third to a half of the populations of the affluent West, including Europe and the USA, are thought to have diverticula, or small 'pouches' in the outer layer of their bowel, although most, perhaps 70 per cent of those, have no symptoms. The unlucky ones experience pain, bloating and either diarrhoea or constipation. If the diverticula become inflamed, the condition is known as diverticulitis and may necessitate a stay in hospital and even surgery.

It is thought that the development of diverticula may be a result of our over-refined, fibre-poor, modern diets, since the condition is much less prevalent in the developing world where people consume more fibre and tend to produce larger, bulkier stools.

Diverticular disease is equally common in men and women and tends to affect older people more than the young. Symptoms include pain, often on the lower left-hand side of the abdomen, irregular bowel habits and pellet-like motions resembling 'rabbit droppings'. It is thought that a healthy diet with plenty of fruit and vegetables can help prevent this condition, but once established, changing the diet does not always help. Drugs, including the kind of anti-spasmodics also prescribed for the colicky spasms common in irritable bowel syndrome, can be effective. If surgery is needed, about two-thirds of patients will regain normal bowel function; in other cases a colostomy may be necessary.

Pancreatitis

As its name suggests, this is inflammation of the pancreas, which as we have already seen, is a vital organ in the digestive system. Like many other conditions, the main symptom is acute pain in the upper abdomen, often accompanied by nausea and vomiting. In acute pancreatitis, this pain comes on suddenly and becomes extremely severe, often spreading to the back. Fever may also be present.

A related condition is chronic pancreatitis, in which the patient is in constant pain and often loses weight as eating makes the pain worse. Also, a damaged and inflamed pancreas is not able to do its job in producing the necessary enzymes to help digest food. The most common cause of chronic pancreatitis is excess alcohol consumption and doctors are becoming increasingly concerned that the UK's binge-drinking culture is leading to this condition becoming more widespread.

It is not known exactly why excessive alcohol consumption causes pancreatitis. The acute form of the disease is sometimes caused by gallstones becoming stuck in the bile duct, preventing pancreatic juices from reaching the parts of the digestive system where they are needed. A tendency to pancreatitis sometimes runs in families. High blood fats, parasitic infections, or injury are also occasional causes.

Someone with pancreatitis is obviously very ill and needs hospital attention. Blood tests, ultrasounds or CT scans can confirm the diagnosis. Treatments include painkillers and antibiotics, plus advice on giving up smoking and drinking. There may be complications such as kidney failure, diabetes or even pancreatic cancer.

Cancers of the digestive tract

Like other parts of the body, the digestive tract can be the site of cancers – among them cancers of the gullet (oesophagus), stomach, pancreas and bowel. Even today, the development of the 200 or so different diseases, affecting many organs and tissues of the body, which we call cancer, is not completely understood. However, much more is known about the causes and treatments than was the case even ten or 20 years ago.

Cancer begins when one of the body's cells begins to divide in an uncontrolled way, eventually forming a lump or tumour. Some tumours then grow to damage surrounding healthy organs and tissues, and in other cases cancer cells break away and spread to other parts of the body.

We know that the development of cancers can be affected by genetic factors, hormones, immune conditions and also environmental factors such as exposure to poisons like alcohol and nicotine, chemical agents, radiation, infection with viruses and bacteria, and poor diet. Age is an important factor. The vast majority of those who develop cancers of the digestive tract are over 50, although that doesn't, of course, mean that younger people can afford to ignore symptoms.

For reasons we don't yet understand, cancer of the oesophagus, or gullet, is becoming much more common. Men are more at risk than women, and as with most cancers, older people are more likely to develop this condition. Other risk factors include smoking, drinking excess alcohol, being overweight or obese, and experiencing persistent gastric reflux or heartburn (see Chapter 3). Eating a lot of pickled or smoked foods – as people do in Central Asia and China – also seems to be a risk factor.

Symptoms include difficulty in swallowing, weight loss without dieting, pain in the throat, hoarseness or a persistent cough, and persistent hiccups or vomiting. All these could, of course, be symptoms of much less serious illness but if they worsen or recur, it's a sensible precaution to consult your GP. Blood tests, an endoscopy (where a narrow tube with a tiny camera on the end is passed down the throat so that the oesophagus can be examined) and a barium swallow (see p. 90) are the usual methods of diagnosis. Treatment, as with most cancers, may be by surgery, radiation or chemotherapy drugs (see Chapter 10).

Stomach cancer, by contrast, is only about one-third as common as it was 50 years ago. The reasons for this fall in the number of cases are not known. One theory is that food now tends to be refrigerated for storage, rather than being smoked or pickled as it was in the days before refrigeration became commonplace. Men are twice as likely to develop stomach cancer as women and there is also a higher risk in people who have *H. pylori*, the bacterium which is implicated in many cases of stomach or duodenal ulcer. Family history also seems to be a risk factor, as are smoking and a poor diet. We shall be looking at stomach-friendly diets in the next chapter, but milk, fresh vegetables and vitamin C have all been suggested as sensible preventative measures. For some time now the Government has been recommending the 'five-a-day' rule but it seems that only about one in six women in the UK are actually eating their five portions of fruit and veg every day. It's thought to be the antioxidants in fruit and veg which have a protective effect.

Stomach cancer produces the same symptoms as many other, less serious, digestive disorders – indigestion, pain, bloating, lack of appetite, unexplained weight loss, nausea and vomiting, blood in the stools. As always, the advice from the medical profession is that if these symptoms are persistent, recurring and/or severe, go to your GP. The chances are that you will be diagnosed with something much less alarming than any form of cancer, but if you do have cancer, the sooner it is diagnosed and treated, the more favourable the outcome is likely to be. Treatment for stomach cancer is likely to involve surgery and chemotherapy.

Pancreatic cancer is hard to diagnose, as the pancreas is situated deep within the body and symptoms sometimes do not appear until the condition is quite advanced. They also tend to vary according to where the tumour is located in the organ and which of its functions are affected. Pain in the abdomen and/or back, bowel problems, loss of appetite and jaundice can all be warning signs. Because it is difficult to diagnose, the outlook for treatment is not particularly good at present. It is sometimes possible to remove the tumour surgically and research into drug treatments is ongoing. A drug called gemcitabine is often prescribed and combinations of this drug with other drugs and other anti-cancer treatments are currently being trialled.

Bowel cancer or colon cancer is the country's second most

common cancer. It's the disease which killed World Cup hero Bobby Moore and popular TV presenter Helen Rollason. It affects both men and women equally and, most importantly, is both preventable and treatable, if caught in time. CORE, Cancer Research UK, and specialized cancer charities like Bowel Cancer UK (contact details on pp. 114 and 115) are extremely eager to make us all more 'colon aware' so that we know what to look for and don't delay asking for help out of either ignorance or embarrassment.

Prevention of bowel cancer has been summed up as the Three B's – better diet, being fit, and bowel awareness. Researchers estimate that the numbers of cases of bowel cancer could be cut by as many as 50 per cent if we had healthier diets. Physical exercise may not be the first thing you think of when you are considering cancer prevention, but being active is known to help. And bowel awareness means that you should not ignore the following symptoms:

- change in bowel habit which is unusual for you (either diarrhoea or constipation or a switch from one to the other) and which lasts longer than a few days;
- blood and/or mucus in the stools;
- abdominal pain and tenderness;
- a feeling that your bowel is not emptying completely;
- weight loss without dieting;
- excessive fatigue.

Bowel Cancer UK suggest that you keep a diary of your symptoms for a couple of weeks, noting when and how often you have pain, bleeding or bowel movements. If the symptoms persist, go to your GP. Tests for bowel cancer usually take place in hospital and include sigmoidoscopy or colonoscopy, where narrow instruments are passed gently into the back passage to see what is happening there. Tissue samples can then be taken for analysis. We shall be looking at hospital tests and treatments in more detail in Chapters 9 and 10.

It is important to remember that bowel cancer is one of the most curable forms of the disease, as long as it is caught and treated at an early stage. Tumours treated when they are still localized – which means before they have had a chance to spread – have a 90 per cent chance of a cure.

5

Looking after your digestive system

'You are what you eat', or so they say! Food is fuel for the body, and you can't expect to be, or remain healthy, if you don't choose the right kind of fuel.

On the whole, we aren't very kind to our insides in Britain. Many of us, especially women, have a mixed-up attitude to food. Because of the relentless pressure from the media, and from other women, to stay slim, we tend to think of food as slightly 'naughty' instead of something to be savoured and enjoyed. Sadly, though, however much we might admire and look up to skinny celebrities, all the evidence points to the fact that the British are getting fatter. Too many of us exist on a diet of junk food, chips and fatty snacks, cakes and sweets. We don't linger for hours over plates of home-cooked pasta and salad as they do on the Continent. Many of us prefer to grab a sandwich at our office desk (the average lunch 'hour' in Britain now lasts approximately nineteen minutes). We end the day popping a high-fat, high-salt ready meal into the microwave or sending out for a pizza or Indian or Chinese takeaway, often last thing at night.

Then we wonder why we suffer from digestive problems. The British don't have a reputation for being proud of our native cuisine. Ask a foreigner and they will probably associate 'English food' with something like roast beef, or fish and chips – that's if they are not shuddering at our tradition of soggy over-cooked vegetables or greasy fried breakfasts. This chapter is about eating to be kind to your digestive system, and convincing yourself that healthy eating doesn't have to be dull or mean denying yourself treats. Instead, eating well involves tucking in to as much as you like of fresh, healthy, preferably home-prepared and home-cooked food. A meal should leave you feeling satisfied rather than uncomfortable, bloated and knowing that you will be tossing and turning half the night with indigestion, or knocking back the antacids because you have yet another upset stomach.

Eating the right kind of food in the right way will not only help to avoid everyday digestive problems like heartburn and constipation, it can also help to prevent some of the more serious conditions, like digestive cancers. It is estimated that anything from one-quarter to one-third of cancers are caused by bad diet, including, not surprisingly, many of the digestive cancers we looked at in the last chapter. A report from the World Cancer Research Fund in November 2007, based on the findings of a panel of 21 experts in diet, nutrition and public health, said that obese people run as great a risk of getting cancer as smokers, and recommended a diet rich in plant foods and low in red meat.

So, if you want to keep your digestive system in the best possible shape, what should you be eating, and is there anything you should be avoiding? CORE says that most people's digestive systems can cope with the occasional blow-out or indulgence, and with the huge variety of foods that form part of the modern diet. However, too many unwise food choices can lead to problems in the future. We all know people who seem to have iron digestions, just as there are people who never seem to get hangovers however much they drink, but most of us are less lucky.

From the point of view of general digestive health, there are three main diet tips:

- eat less fat, especially saturated fats;
- eat plenty of fruit and vegetables – the Government's 'five-a-

day' recommendation is a good starting point, though there is no reason why you shouldn't eat more than this;

- make sure you eat plenty of fibre or 'roughage' – the part of food which doesn't actually get digested but passes through the system, stimulating the digestive tract and helping to prevent constipation.

The truth about fats

Fats should form no more than about one-third of your calorie intake, rather than the 40-plus percentage contained in the 'average British diet'. You do need some fats, but it's best to stick to the 'healthier' ones such as mono- or poly-unsaturated fats. These can be found in products like some margarines (check the label), oily fish, plant oils, avocados, olive oil, peanuts and almonds.

Fats to be avoided are the 'saturated' types, mostly found in meat and animal-derived products like milk, cream and butter, many of which are solid at room temperature. Some vegetable fats like coconut oil and palm oil are also very high in saturated fats. Steer clear of 'trans fats' too. These are often found in processed foods like shop-bought cakes and biscuits and are sometimes labelled 'hydrogenated fats' or 'trans-fatty acids'. They are formed when vegetable oils are subjected to a chemical process called hydrogenation.

These days it isn't particularly difficult to cut down on the fat in your diet. Every supermarket sells low- or reduced-fat products and many of them are just as palatable as the fatty alternatives. To cut down on fat:

- Grill or bake food instead of frying it. If you do fry, use the smallest possible amount of olive oil instead of a 'hard' fat like lard.
- Trim visible fat off meat and the skin off poultry.

- Always choose low-fat versions of dairy products like cheese and yoghurt.
- Snack on nuts and dried fruit rather than crisps and chocolate.
- Keep cakes and biscuits as occasional treats rather than everyday items. You can even bake your own.
- If you really can't resist butter, spread it thinly and avoid adding a knob of butter to your vegetables.
- Use semi-skimmed milk instead of the full-fat version.

Love your veg!

It's really rather sad that so few of us are currently managing to eat five portions a day of fruit and vegetables. It's probably because there are still so many people who can only associate vegetables with the sort of soggy cabbage served up as off-white sludge at old-fashioned school dinners, or 'salads' which consist of a bit of limp lettuce and half a tomato. Imaginatively presented, cooked and served, vegetables and fruit can look and be absolutely delicious as well as good for you. Learn to experiment with all the varieties in the shops and markets and you won't have any trouble reaching your five-a-day target.

A simple way to achieve it is to have a glass of orange juice (or apple juice, or cranberry, or anything else you fancy – or maybe a fruit smoothie?) with your breakfast. If you have cereal, chop up a couple of dried apricots, figs and prunes and add them to the mix. Have a banana or a handful of grapes as a mid-morning snack.

If you have a sandwich at lunchtime, pack it with salad leaves in addition to your favourite meat, fish, cheese or egg filling. Experiment with different leaves including the strongly flavoured ones like rocket and watercress as well as endive, lamb's lettuce, chopped red cabbage, spinach or lollo rosso. Better still, make yourself a tasty mixed salad to eat at your desk and add even more interesting vegetables, like sweetcorn, chopped beets, grated carrot, celery – the choice is endless. Add chopped fresh herbs like parsley, mint or basil for even more flavour.

Then a couple of helpings of lightly cooked vegetables with your evening meal, with perhaps a fruit salad to follow, or some strawberries or raspberries (in summer) or a dried fruit or black-berry-and-apple compote later in the year. That's easily more than five a day for very little extra effort.

If you're cooking for the family, remember that the five-a-day rule applies to them, too. One tip for getting your kids to enjoy their greens is to allow them to grow their own! Yes, really. Schools which have gardening clubs report that even the most reluctant veg-eaters are much more enthusiastic if they've seen their carrots or lettuce grown from tiny plants or seeds. Growing cress on flannel or a few herbs in a window-box could be a start ...

Why fibre matters

Unlike the other nutrients which are essential for good health, fibre doesn't contain any protein, vitamins or minerals, but it still has an important role to play in a digestion-friendly diet. Fibre is the part of plant foods which human beings cannot digest. The technical term is 'non-starch polysaccharide' and fibre is also commonly referred to as 'roughage'.

Fibre in foods stimulates the digestive tract and helps it to function properly. It promotes the presence of 'good' bacteria in the colon and softens bowel motions, making them easier to pass and preventing constipation. It is thought to slow down the absorption of carbohydrates in food, helping meals to seem more satisfying, so it also has a role to play in weight control.

Fibre is found in fruit, including the skins, peel and pips, veg-etables, pulses like beans, peas and lentils, oats, barley and seeds, as well as wholegrain cereals.

As well as helping to prevent everyday digestive problems like constipation by getting a sluggish gut moving, there is increasing evidence that a high-fibre diet can help to prevent serious disease like colon cancer. Health experts usually recommend a diet that includes about 30 g of fibre – from a variety of sources – every day. As with fruit and vegetable intake, it is not especially difficult to increase the amount of fibre you are eating. If you keep to the five-a-day rule, you will be getting more fibre anyway. Eat more wholegrain bread and high-fibre breakfast cereals (containing at least 5 g of fibre per serving). Instead of white rice, flour and pasta, use the brown and wholemeal varieties: they have far more flavour anyway. Snacks such as nuts and raisins, dried fruit, and wholemeal biscuits can also increase your fibre intake.

Cut down on white bread, rice and pasta and over-processed, pre-prepared foods as they generally have a lower fibre content than the wholegrain varieties.

Remember that if you are increasing the amount of fibre in your diet it's important to increase the amount of water or non-alcoholic liquids that you drink, too. The point about fibre is that it absorbs a lot of liquid, increasing the weight and size of your bowel motions and the pressure on the bowel wall. This helps your lower bowel to do its job properly, but if you don't drink plenty of liquid, the result can be hard, dry stools and uncomfortable constipation. Recommended amounts of water do vary, but it seems likely that most of us are not drinking anything like enough to keep our insides in good working order! Six cups or glasses of water, diluted fruit juice or fruit tea per day should be the absolute minimum, and more if you can manage it. A good rule is to drink a glass of water every time you pass the kitchen sink or the office water-cooler to keep your system healthy.

If you already have digestive problems

You may need to adjust your diet accordingly. Ask your GP's advice or get a referral to a dietitian. For example, although some people with irritable bowel syndrome benefit from a high-fibre diet, others find it makes their symptoms worse. Most people know from experience what they can and can't eat and which foods upset them; it's simply common sense to avoid spicy foods, acid fruits, shellfish, strawberries or whatever it is that always 'disagrees' with you.

In recent years it has become fashionable in some quarters to blame digestive upsets on food allergy, or food intolerance, and we shall be looking at this possibility in Chapter 8. Conventional medical wisdom at the moment states that many more people believe they are 'allergic' to certain foods than is actually the case. Of course, if you have actually been diagnosed with a condition like coeliac disease (see previous chapter) then you will know that you have to adjust your diet to exclude all foods containing gluten. If you have not had a definite diagnosis, however, it can be unwise to put yourself on a faddy 'exclusion diet' (for example, excluding wheat and/or dairy products) except under proper medical supervision.

The reason for this is simple. Everyone, whatever the state of their digestive system, needs a balanced diet with a reasonable intake of foods from all the main food groups – protein, carbohydrates, fats, vitamins and minerals. Eating a limited or restricted diet, even if you are eating basically healthy foods – green vegetables, for instance – is not good for you. Foods need to nourish your body alongside other foods and it may be the balance of proteins, vitamins, carbohydrates and minerals that keeps your digestion healthy. So don't restrict yourself. Enjoy experimenting with different types of bread – wholemeal and granary rolls, rye bread, bagels, fruit and savoury breads – as well as the great variety of vegetables and fruit, meats and fish and pulses available.

It is simply not yet known whether some of the substances which are thought to keep our digestive systems healthy and prevent serious diseases like cancer developing work by themselves, or as part of whole foods and a balanced diet. This means it is generally better to obtain vitamin C, which is thought to protect against oesophageal and stomach cancers, from fruit and vegetables than from supplements. Vitamin C is found in citrus fruits, strawberries, broccoli, spring greens and green peppers. Vitamin E, found in wholegrain breads and cereals and unsaturated vegetable oils, may have a similar protective effect.

The mineral selenium is also thought to protect against cancer, but is needed by the body in very small quantities. Selenium is found in brazil nuts, wholemeal bread, seafood, and sunflower seeds.

Far-Eastern countries, where people eat a lot of pickled and smoked foods, tend to have higher rates of digestive cancers, which suggests that these foods are best eaten in moderation. Chinese people, who eat a lot of heavily smoked and salted fish, have a rate of oesophageal cancer which is roughly ten times ours. Barbecuing also creates cancer-causing substances on the surface of foods. That doesn't mean that you can't enjoy the occasional barbecue or both smoked foods and pickles, but it is something to bear in mind. Researchers are learning a lot about which foods are best for the digestion by looking at the different eating patterns in various countries. The European Prospective Investigation of Cancer (EPIC) study is a long-term research project looking at 500,000 people in ten European countries to work out the relationship between diet and cancer. So far, the research has indicated that

- high fibre intakes reduce the risk of bowel cancer;
- eating a lot of red or processed meat increases the risk of stomach and bowel cancer;
- fish may reduce the risk of bowel cancer;

- being overweight or obese increases the risk of oesophageal cancer;
- 'apple-shaped' people with a large waist-to-hip ratio run a higher risk of pancreatic cancer.
- milk, cheese and calcium are linked to a reduced risk of bowel cancer.

Research into the cancer-preventing properties of various foods is ongoing, but the general advice is still that a balanced diet rich in fruit and vegetables is the best bet. A study from Ohio State University in August 2007 suggested that a class of antioxidant compounds known as anthocyanins, which give fruits and vegetables like blueberries, radishes and red cabbage their colour, may have a protective effect against colon cancer.

How we eat matters, too!

Eating for a healthy digestive system is not just a matter of what we eat, but also *how* we eat. A recent survey for indigestion remedy Bisodol found that less than 40 per cent of us sit at a table every day to eat our main meal, and that more than three-quarters eat a main meal in under twenty minutes!

None of this is great news for our digestions. Professor Colette Short, Director of Science at Yakult, says that it is important to

- take your time over meals. The sight and smell of food stimulates your digestive juices. Kick-start your digestive system by relaxing before you eat;
- sit down, make yourself comfortable and give your digestive system a helping hand. Avoid eating on the move;
- break down every mouthful into small pieces by chewing it well, which will ensure that your food is processed efficiently. Eat slowly to be sure all the goodness is extracted. If you gorge you may overload your system.

Cancer Research UK has further tips:

- Keep to the same eating pattern every day, for meals and snacks, and have regular mealtimes.
- Focus on food while you're eating, rather than on the TV or work. This will help you to eat less.
- Eat slowly. It takes time for your body to register that you are full.

Probiotics – why they are important

We hear a lot about 'probiotic' yoghurts and 'health' drinks like Yakult and Actimel. But what are these probiotics and what can they do for our digestive health?

Chapter 2 described how the human colon is home to millions and millions of bacteria. The 'friendly' bacteria in the gut are a vital part of our digestive systems as they help to prevent infection and also help the gut to break down and absorb the nutrients in the food we eat. Upsetting the balance of these bacteria – as sometimes happens if, for example, you have been prescribed a course of antibiotics, can lead to diarrhoea and difficulty absorbing food. Probiotics basically repopulate the gut with healthy, friendly bacteria.

That is the theory at least, although the jury is still out on this one as far as the medical establishment is concerned. People have been eating 'live' yoghurt for health reasons for hundreds of years. It was 100 years ago that a pathologist named Metchikoff noticed that Bulgarian peasants all seemed to live very long and healthy lives. He attributed this to the fact that they drank a lot of fermented milk products – in other words, probiotics.

There is some evidence that probiotics can improve digestive health in some people. Glenn Gibson, Professor of Food Microbiology at Reading University, recommends them as a protection against disease-causing bacteria such as *E. coli* and

Campylobacter. It is known that people over 60 have fewer friendly bacteria in their systems so may benefit from a top-up with a probiotic product. Some experts believe that for best results you would also need to eat the right foods for the friendly bacteria to feed on, for instance onions, leeks, garlic, chicory and artichoke, so-called 'prebiotics'.

To be genuinely beneficial, probiotics must be the right kind – lactobacillus or bifidobacteria – and they must be able to survive the digestive process in order actually to reach the colon – including surviving the strong acids in the stomach! A study at the Royal Free Hospital in London found that only 14 out of 39 advertised products really worked. Those that worked included the best-known names like Yakult, Actimel and Danone as well as the Multibionta supplements. If you choose to take probiotics, it might be worth getting in touch with the manufacturers and finding out what scientific evidence they have that their products really do work.

In October 2007 a new probiotic supplement called VSL–3 was launched which actually combines six different types of beneficial bacteria, including *Streptococcus thermophilus*, bifidobacteria and four different types of lactobacillus. As well as protecting the inner layer of the gut from damaging bacteria, it is claimed that this product helps to heal inflammation and prevent 'leaks' from the intestinal cells. Unlike some of the other products on the market, this one has actually been through at least two double-blind, placebo-controlled clinical trials in which all those in the trial (around 75 patients) with irritable bowel syndrome found it effective. A spokesperson for The Gut Trust said that any new product that helped people manage their IBS was to be welcomed, and at least one consultant gastroenterologist said that in this area where medical opinion varies so much, it now seems that a mixture of concentrated strains of probiotic bacteria can be of some benefit.

Food hygiene

One of the most effective ways of making sure that your digestive system remains healthy is by following simple food hygiene precautions, whether in your own home and kitchen, in restaurants and cafés, or on holiday abroad.

It's not known exactly how many cases of food poisoning there are in the UK every year because many people don't go to the doctor and regard an episode of diarrhoea, sickness and stomach cramps as 'just one of those things'. But it doesn't have to be. Food poisoning is unpleasant and often avoidable. The very young, the elderly and pregnant women are particularly vulnerable.

The basic rules of kitchen hygiene include:

- Always wash your hands before preparing food.
- Make sure all utensils, chopping boards and cleaning cloths are really clean. Never use the same utensils for raw and cooked food.
- Don't let raw food drip on to cooked food (for instance in the fridge). Store raw meat and poultry in sealed containers at the bottom of the fridge.
- Thaw meat and poultry thoroughly before cooking and check that it is cooked through before serving.
- Only re-heat food once and *again*, check it is thoroughly cooked.
- Follow the instructions on ready-prepared and packaged foods. Be aware of the difference between 'best before' and 'use by' dates. 'Best before' means that you can continue to eat the food safely after the date given, but there may be some reduction in quality. 'Use by' means that the food should not be eaten after the date given.
- Put food that needs to be kept cool straight into the fridge when you come in from the shops.
- Cool cooked food quickly, then refrigerate it.

- Don't overload the fridge.
- Wash pets' dishes separately. Don't allow pets on to surfaces where food is prepared.
- Take care with picnic and barbecued food – there are more cases of food poisoning in summer.
- Carry picnic food in insulated coolbags and don't leave it lying about in hot weather.
- Keep raw and cooked meats for barbecues separate. Use separate utensils for raw and cooked foods and make absolutely sure barbecued food is cooked through, not charred on the outside and raw inside. Throw away any food left out for more than two hours in hot weather.

Holiday tummy

'Gyppy tummy', 'Montezuma's Revenge' and 'Delhi belly' are just some of the names given to the upset stomachs so many experience when on holiday. A change of diet, contaminated water, and an excess of sun and alcohol, can all be blamed for the conditions which can easily ruin a two-week break. So how can they be avoided?

Prevention is always better than cure and you can help yourself by using your common sense. Remember that the sun is hotter than you are used to and that unfamiliar food and drink can upset you, so take it easy to start with. Pick your destination carefully. You're more likely to run into problems in the developing world than you are in Northern Europe, the USA or Australia. When you are abroad:

- stick to freshly cooked and thoroughly cooked food and avoid re-heated food left standing at room temperature, especially in hot climates;
- only drink bottled water from sealed containers and avoid having ice in drinks. Use bottled water for cleaning your teeth and washing fruit and vegetables if you are self-catering.

If you're really off the beaten track, you should take water-purifying tablets;

- wash your hands thoroughly after using the toilet and before preparing food;
- avoid raw foods, unpeeled fruit and salads;
- if you are struck down, drink plenty of plain fluids like bottled water or flat cola drinks to avoid dehydration. If you can face food stick to plain boiled rice, clear soup or bananas;
- always pack some anti-diarrhoea medication (e.g. Imodium) in your first aid kit.

Exercise and digestive health

Looking after your digestive system is not just a matter of what and how you eat. Exercise is important, too. Keeping fit and active will help a sluggish gut to get moving. It is known that keeping fit and maintaining a healthy weight can reduce your risk of the most common digestive cancers, such as bowel cancer. According to Cancer Research UK, at least 50 scientific studies have shown that being active can roughly halve your risk of colon cancer.

This isn't just because active people are less likely to be overweight or obese, also risk factors for cancer. It may be because activity helps you to have regular bowel movements, so that cancer-causing substances in food pass through your bowel more quickly. It may also be because being active reduces the levels of insulin, some hormones and some growth factors which encourage the growth of tumours when present at high levels, or because activity reduces bowel inflammation which might otherwise lead to bowel cancer.

Being overweight is also a risk factor for other digestive problems, ranging from heartburn and acid reflux to gallstones. It really is worthwhile making sure you are a healthy weight for your height and incorporating at least 30 minutes of exercise a day into your lifestyle. You don't have to join a gym or take up jogging if you don't fancy the idea. Instead, make exercise part of your everyday life by walking at least part of the way to work, using the stairs instead of the lift, shopping on foot rather than by car and putting plenty of effort into housework and gardening. Walking is free, easy and suitable for all the family and it benefits your heart and lungs as well as your digestive system.

With the London Olympics coming up we are all going to become more sport-conscious. There are so many activities available that there must be something you would enjoy. Indoors or out-of-doors, alone, with a friend or in a team or group, why not try keep-fit, aerobics, step classes, trampolining, fencing, basketball, badminton, tennis, swimming, aqua-aerobics, women's football or rugby, ballroom dancing, line-dancing, salsa, country- or folk-dancing, golf, cycling, rambling, spinning, Pilates, power-walking, dry-slope ski-ing, Nordic walking, Boxercise, kick-boxing, martial arts, rollerblading, snowboarding, hockey, skateboarding, ballet, Fitball, rowing, netball, disco or jazz dance, ice-skating, body conditioning, skipping, squash, hiking, pole-dancing, British Military Fitness, Slimnastics, lacrosse, table-tennis, climbing, scuba-diving, snorkelling or exercising to a fitness video by your favourite celebrity?!

6

The enemies of digestive health

In the last chapter, we looked at what individuals can do to keep their digestive systems in good order, including eating the right things in the right way, following sensible food-hygiene precautions and getting plenty of exercise.

There are some habits which are best avoided if you want a healthy digestive system, not to mention if you want to keep the rest of your body in tip-top condition! These include health enemy Number One – smoking – and drinking alcohol, which also has an effect on digestive health.

Smoking

Ever since the link between smoking and lung cancer was established in the 1960s, the Government and health educationalists have been trying to persuade us all to give up the deadly weed. The latest attempt to discourage smoking, including the 24 per cent of British women who still smoke, came in July 2007, when the habit was banned in all enclosed spaces, including clubs, bars, pubs and restaurants. It's too early to say as yet how much effect this will have on the number of smokers, but it's hoped that making smoking more difficult and less acceptable socially will at least make those who still smoke think harder about giving up.

It's worth remembering that it isn't just your lungs which are affected when you smoke. Few of the body's systems and organs are *not* affected by the cigarette habit, according to health campaigners ASH (Action on Smoking and Health). If you can, think back to your first-ever cigarette. If you're like most women who smoke, that first puff was probably shared with friends behind the bike sheds at school and made you feel ever so daring and wickedly grown-up. What else did it make you feel, though? Probably, if you're honest, dizzy and nauseous. You may even have thrown up – a lot of first-time smokers do. That's because cigarettes are poisonous. Believe it or not they contain as many as 4,000 chemical compounds and at least 400 toxins. These include:

- nicotine, which as well as being at least as addictive as heroin, is a potent poison which is used in insecticides and raises the body's cholesterol levels, altering the balance between 'good' and 'bad' cholesterol;
- carbon monoxide, a poisonous gas which can kill if it's inhaled in large amounts;
- tar, a known carcinogen (cancer-causing substance);
- acetone, the chemical used in nail-varnish remover;
- ammonia, also found in cleaning fluids;
- arsenic, a deadly poison;
- benzene, which is used as a solvent in fuel;
- ethanol, the chemical used in anti-freeze;
- formaldehyde, the chemical sometimes used in the preservation of dead bodies;
- assorted other deadly poisons.

Small wonder that your digestion, all the way along your alimentary canal from your mouth to your lower bowel, can be affected by this cocktail of dangerous chemicals.

Smoking kills about 114,000 people a year in the UK but it also contributes to many non-fatal but unpleasant and debilitating illnesses, including digestive illnesses. About 364,000 hospital admissions – that's about 1,000 a day – are estimated to be smoking-related. Among the non-fatal digestive conditions which are caused or made worse by smoking are heartburn and acid reflux problems, stomach and duodenal ulcers, and polyps in the colon. Smokers have about four times the risk of developing Crohn's disease (see pp. 26–7) of non-smokers. Very few non-smokers get mouth or throat cancer and again, the risk for smokers is about four times higher. Cigarette smoke seems to irritate the oesophagus, increase acid production in the stomach and damage the protective mucus which lines the stomach, which explains why smokers are more at risk of heartburn and ulcer-type conditions.

Stomach, liver and pancreatic cancers are also more common in smokers.

Time to give up?

Most women who smoke – eight out of ten by some estimates – want to give up. Not only is it an unhealthy habit but it's expensive and ruins your looks. The days when every glamorous movie star was photographed with a cigarette between her lips are long gone. Today's smokers are more likely to look like Vicky Pollard than Kate Moss. Maybe you have tried before and failed, but that doesn't mean it's not worth trying again. There are plenty of people who can help you. Ask your GP about local Stop Smoking clinics, or call the NHS Stop Smoking Helpline (contact details on p. 116) or QUIT (contact details on p. 116.)

In order to give up successfully, you will need to be motivated (no one can do it for you!) so ask yourself why and when you smoke. Maybe it's because

- you think it helps you to relax;
- you think it keeps you slim;
- it gives you ten minutes of 'me time', a little treat just for you, away from the demands of your job and/or family;
- it's just a habit – you automatically light up when you have a cuppa, or when you're out with friends.

Once you have worked out what smoking does for you, it should be easier to work out how you can achieve the same effect without the fags. If you need to relax, take a look at some of the stress-busting tips on pages 68 to 70 and try them instead. Experts say that in reality, far from relaxing you, nicotine actually just damps down the nicotine cravings.

Smokers often do put on a little weight when they give up – it can change your metabolism or you might eat more because your food is no longer flavoured with cigarette smoke – but if you follow the healthy eating guidelines in the previous chapter, this should not be a problem. Any initial weight gain soon stabilizes. If smoking is just a habit, change your routine a little – relax with a magazine or the TV instead of a cigarette, take a different route to work that doesn't pass the tobacconist's, or fiddle with a biro or worry beads if you need something to do with your hands.

There is a lot of practical help for quitters too. Stop Smoking clinics often offer a combination of drug help using new drugs like Zyban (buproprion hydrochloride), counselling to help you deal with cravings and nicotine replacement therapy which can be very effective. Some people find that complementary treatments like hypnotherapy or acupuncture are effective though there doesn't seem to be much scientific evidence supporting this. Above all, as with all addictions, you really have to want to change your life. At the end of the day, it's what works for you – perhaps the thought of being able to spend the £1,700 a year you'll save, as a 20-a-day smoker, on a really fabulous holiday, or the thought of starting a new year – or a new relationship – smoke-free. You will lower your risk of lung cancer and heart disease, and your digestive health will also benefit, not only now but in the future.

Alcohol

The figures for women and alcohol misuse are beginning to look frightening, not just to the Government and the medical profession who have to pick up the pieces, but to the rest of us too. The main findings of the 2001 General Household Survey were that one in ten women admitted to 'binge-drinking' – which means drinking more than twice the recommended safe limit, on at least one day per week. And a staggering one in three younger women drink more than they should, in other words more than 14 units of alcohol a week. It's estimated that the beleaguered NHS has to spend a whopping £2 billion on alcohol-related disease every year.

It should come as no surprise that it's the digestive system which suffers most from heavy or binge-drinking. Most alcoholic drinks contain congeners, impurities which increase the poisoning effect. The 'hangover' most of us are all too familiar with is just another name for poisoning-plus-dehydration, which results in a pounding head and an upset stomach, with more serious damage done to the digestive system in the long term. The World Cancer Research Fund report of November 2007, referred to in the previous chapter, also reminded us that sticking to the Government's safe-drinking limits is important in cancer prevention.

Know your limits

You don't have to be an 'alcoholic' to suffer from the effects of alcohol. Safe limits for drinking are actually much lower than many women realize – just 14 'units' of alcohol per week, or no more than 2 or 3 small drinks a day. What's more, it's recommended that you have at least a couple of alcohol-free days every week to give your system a chance to rest. How you drink matters, as well. That 'binge-drinking' which we currently hear so much about, involving drinking more than five or six alcoholic drinks per session, is most damaging to women's health.

1 unit of alcohol is 10 ml, which means that
1 pint of strong lager = 3 units

1 pint of ordinary lager, beer or cider = 2 units
1 175 ml glass of wine = 2 units
1 alcopop = 1.5 units
1 measure of spirits = 1 unit

It is also important to remember that many wines are 11 or 12 per cent alcohol, so a small glass will give you 1.5 units of alcohol. If you drink at home, remember that bottled lagers and ciders are generally stronger than draught.

The body breaks down alcohol at a rate of about one unit per hour, but exactly how fast will depend on all kinds of factors, including your weight, your age, your metabolism, your stress levels, whether you have recently eaten, where you are in your monthly cycle and whether you are on medication. Generally speaking, though, if you keep your drinking at or below the recommended levels you are unlikely to suffer any health problems from it. However if you regularly drink more than three units a day, and especially if you binge-drink, your health will be affected.

How alcohol affects women

Like everything else you eat and drink, alcohol is processed by your digestive system – which is why your digestion suffers if you drink too much. One-fifth to one quarter of a shot of alcohol is absorbed from the stomach and the rest from the small intestine. Once in the bloodstream, the alcohol is carried to the liver where detoxification begins. The liver is responsible for eliminating about 95 per cent of the alcohol from the body; the rest is eliminated via your breath, sweat, urine, faeces and saliva.

Generally speaking, lighter people are affected by alcohol more quickly than heavier ones. And this is an area where equality of the sexes just doesn't apply. Because women's bodies are smaller than men's, with the average woman weighing 58 kg against a man's 70 kg, women are at a health disadvantage when it comes to drinking. Women carry 10 per cent more body fat and a higher proportion of fat to water, so alcohol travels around the female body in a more concentrated form and is more harmful. Women also have lower levels of an enzyme called 'alcohol dehydrogenase' which normally breaks down alcohol, so it takes women's livers longer to process it. This all adds up to the fact that women are more vulnerable to alcohol-related diseases. As well as the proportion of body fat, recent research from the USA has suggested that the way women's stomachs break down alcohol may also be a factor.

How alcohol affects the digestive system

It won't be news to anyone who has ever had a hangover that alcohol can upset the stomach, causing sickness and diarrhoea. This is because alcohol irritates the lining of the stomach and intestine. It also increases the blood flow to these organs, which increases the secretion of stomach acid. In its turn, this can result in heartburn, acid reflux and aggravation or impaired healing of any existing gastric ulcers. Gastritis, the painful condition where the stomach lining becomes inflamed, is often the result of excessive alcohol consumption.

According to the Institute of Alcohol Studies, drinking more than the recommended amount of two units per day will increase your risk of developing mouth and throat cancer. Over-indulging in spirits seems to put you at particular risk of these cancers, which are twice as common in Scotland as in England. There is also a high rate in Normandy where Calvados is the tipple of choice. Most cases of chronic pancreatitis are alcohol-related. Cancers of the lower bowel are also more common in heavy drinkers, as are problems of malabsorption of food and associated malnutrition. Heavy drinkers are rarely healthy eaters; their digestive systems just can't cope and there are few nutrients in alcohol.

As many drinkers know, it's the liver which suffers most from too much alcohol. A TV programme in Channel 4's *Dispatches* series in June 2007 involved a team of liver specialists taking a portable liver unit out on to the streets of London and Birmingham in order to assess the liver health of passers-by. Over half had abnormal readings – in other words, signs of liver damage. These weren't the kind of people most of us would think of as having a problem with drinking.

Liver damage comes in three stages. The first is 'fatty liver disease', which is often found in those drinking just above the safe limits. A healthy liver should contain little or no fat. This can be reversed if you stop drinking. If you continue to drink you may go on to develop alcoholic hepatitis, where the liver becomes puffy, swollen and tender. This can happen after years of heavy drinking, or suddenly, for example after a weekend binge. If your liver fails completely, you can die. Cirrhosis is the final stage of alcoholic liver disease, when the liver is affected by both inflammation and scarring. People who have cirrhosis are more likely than others to develop liver cancer.

Do you have a drink problem?

It isn't easy to face the fact that you have a drink problem, or that all the 'stomach upsets' you get might be the result of excess alcohol consumption. The first step to dealing with any problem you may have is admitting it. Think about your alcohol intake and add up the units you drink over a typical week. The result might surprise you.
You could also try asking yourself

- how much hangovers affect your work performance or your social life;
- if friends or colleagues have annoyed you by criticizing your drinking;
- if you have ever felt guilty about your drinking;
- how often you can't remember what you may have said or done the night before;

- whether you feel you need a drink first thing in the morning to steady your nerves;
- if you can't imagine going out socially without having a drink.

These could all be warning signs that you are drinking more than is good for you. If you are, it could be time to seek help from your GP or an organization such as Alcoholics Anonymous (contact details on p. 114).

Drugs

Very few drugs – either those which can be bought over the counter, or those which are only obtainable on prescription – are totally without side effects. A drug which is easily tolerated and effective in one patient doesn't always work as well for another. Stomach and other digestive problems are common side effects of many kinds of medication. Symptoms can vary from nausea and actual vomiting to constipation, diarrhoea, indigestion and/or heartburn.

Fortunately if a drug you are taking does cause digestive upsets, an alternative is usually available. Always read the patient information leaflet carefully and make sure you understand exactly how and when to take any medication. Some drugs cause problems if taken on an empty stomach so you are advised to take them with or after food, for example.

Many of the most common drugs in use can cause digestive upsets. Aspirin is one example. Although it's a well-established and useful painkiller and is often taken by older people as a preventative measure against heart disease, it is not suitable for everyone and can, in a small percentage of patients (6 per cent) cause indigestion, heartburn, nausea or vomiting. It can cause bleeding in the stomach, as it can damage the stomach lining if taken long term and/or in high doses, especially in older people and those who are already vulnerable, for example those with ulcers. People with these problems are often advised to choose an alternative painkiller, for example paracetamol.

Set against that, there is some evidence from the USA that aspirin can help to protect against bowel cancer. A large research study lasting more than 20 years and looking at 90,000 American nurses found that taking small doses of aspirin – four to six tablets a week – actually had a protective effect against this type of cancer. The highly regarded cancer specialist, Professor Sir Richard Doll, was quoted as saying that people who were at higher-than-average risk of developing bowel cancer might find it useful to take one aspirin every other day. (Those at high risk include people with inflammatory bowel disease or who had previously had bowel, breast, ovarian or endometrial cancer.)

As is often the case with drugs, you need to weigh up the benefits against the possible side effects. Ibuprofen, another common painkiller, can also cause stomach ache and diarrhoea. Some people find codeine has a constipating effect. Antibiotics such as amoxycillin, commonly prescribed for bacterial infections, can also cause diarrhoea. One way of combating this can be to drink probiotic drinks such as Actimel or eat live yoghurt while you are taking the antibiotics. This seems to balance out the effect of the drug and the result is a calmer bowel with no problems.

Nausea and vomiting are common side effects of anti-cancer medication too, although treatment with anti-emetic (sickness) drugs can often be given and dosages are being refined all the time to ensure that patients are given the most effective dose which will destroy the cancer cells.

It goes without saying that street drugs like heroin and cocaine are best avoided for all sorts of reasons, not the least of them being that they can affect your digestion. Nausea and vomiting are common side effects and there is, of course, the possibility that the drug you have been sold has been 'cut' with another substance which may be impure or even poisonous. There is no quality control on illegal pills and potions and you have no way of knowing what you are buying and what effect it will have. Don't risk it.

7

Stress and your digestion

In the last chapter, we looked at lifestyle factors – habits that can affect our digestion, including smoking and drinking. We have also seen that eating the wrong foods at the wrong time can upset the digestive system. Our insides have another enemy, though – stress. It's a popular buzz word in today's world and it is almost fashionable for people to claim they are 'stressed out' but just because it's a cliché doesn't mean it isn't true. It has been estimated that stress-related health problems cost the country a hard-to-believe £7 billion (CBI figures) a year, with 12.8 million working days lost to stress.

So what is stress, exactly, and how does it impact on delicate digestions? Worry, tension and even excitement can all upset the normal workings of our insides. Perhaps surprisingly, happy events as well as obviously worrying ones can cause problems. Going on holiday, moving house or starting a new job may all be welcome changes in your life but they can still be stressful; as, of course, can major worries like divorce, redundancy or bereavement.

Most people have experienced some of the effects of stress on the digestive system at some time in their lives. Exam nerves are a case in point. Few people can go into an examination hall without a few quivers in the stomach and for a lot of GCSE and A-level students, nerves can cause severe stomach upsets. Then there's stage fright, which affects even the most popular, famous and seasoned performers. Singer Barbra Streisand is said not to have given any concerts for 27 years because she suffers from such severe stage fright. Anyone who has had to stand up in front of other people and give a presentation at work or at a social event will have experienced the uneasy feeling of 'but-terflies in the tummy' before they start. Many people find it impossible to speak in public for that reason. That's what stress can do to you. The thoroughly unglamorous-sounding PAD or 'performance-anxiety diarrhoea' is just one of the ways in which stress can affect your digestion.

'There is very little doubt that "functional" digestive disor-ders – those with no organic basis – which are the cause of a lot of ill-health, are affected by stress,' says Dr John Bennett, Chairman of CORE.

> At any gastroenterology clinic, the doctors will see far more patients with that kind of problem than they see patients with organic conditions like inflammatory bowel disease. Two-thirds of gastroenterology work is with functional disorders. They take a lot of time and understanding, and to say that they are 'just' caused by stress is unhelpful.
>
> A British Society of Gastroenterology survey found that dys-pepsia affected 20 to 40 per cent of the population and irritable bowel 20 per cent of the population, which adds up to a lot of people. Of those, 40 per cent said their problem made them avoid activities, 75 per cent had recurrent symptoms, and between 30 and 50 per cent were unable to return to work. So yes, it is a huge problem.
>
> The trouble is that it can be difficult to define 'stress' and the relationship between stress and the digestive problem may not be a direct one. You don't necessarily have an argument with your boss and immediately develop a stomach ache. What we can say is that if someone is leading a stressful life, or going through a bad patch, and they have a propensity to develop digestive problems, stress will make the problem worse. If the person then learns to relax and practises relaxation regularly, it can diminish the severity of the symptoms.

So how does this work? How does stress, either in the form of the pressures and irritations of everyday life, or in the form of a stressful life event, impact on the digestion? The connection between the human brain and the human digestion is a complex one and is being studied by medical researchers worldwide.

They have found that what we all suspected is true, the digestive system is extremely sensitive to mood. That doesn't mean that your stomach pain or IBS is 'all in the mind'. What it does mean is that stress could be at the root of your digestive difficulties. If you go to your GP complaining of constipation, diarrhoea, gastric pain, lack of appetite and/or nausea and are given the usual battery of tests (see Chapter 9 for information about these) you may very well come up with negative results. You may not have an ulcer, still less any more serious digestive disorder – but your symptoms are still there and still perfectly real. This is what Dr Bennett means by a 'functional' disorder, and it will probably make your GP or gastroenterology consultant suspect that stress could be at the root of the problem.

Dr Glenn Gibson, a researcher at the University of Reading School of Food Biosciences says:

> Stress manifests itself most frequently in the GI [gastrointestinal] tract. It does play on the stomach but most of the action is in the intestines.
>
> Food stays in the stomach for about 30 minutes but takes from 48 to 72 hours to pass through the whole of the digestive tract. Stress hormones slow digestion down, leaving food to ferment or stagnate and that can result in diarrhoea or constipation. Stress can also upset the balance of the gut flora which keeps the intestines healthy.

What is stress?

In order to understand what stress might be doing to your digestion you first need to understand what happens to your body when you are stressed. Like animals, we are programmed to react to danger with a physical response known as the 'fight-or-flight syndrome'. If you were a cave-dweller threatened by a sabre-toothed tiger, your only hope would be to bash him over the head with your club or run like hell – or perhaps both. In today's sophisticated world, any kind of threat, from an overdue tax bill to an encounter with a traffic warden, provokes the same sort of physical response. Your nervous system reacts by flooding your body with adrenaline, cortisol and other 'stress hormones' which enable you to fight harder or run faster. Of course, you don't actually intend to either fight or run. If you're suffering from chronic stress, as so many of us are in today's fast-paced world, your fight-or-flight response may be permanently stuck in the 'on' position.

The increase in stress hormones means that your heart beats faster because of the adrenaline, glucose is released into your bloodstream to give you energy and another hormone called corticotropin-releasing hormone or CRH not only increases adrenaline production but also switches off your appetite. When your body perceives danger, it switches off all non-essential functions like digestion, either by slowing the process down or halting it completely. Chronic stress also compromises the immune system, allowing bacteria to get the upper hand, including altering the balance of the bacteria in the gut. The result is upset stomachs with all the associated symptoms of nausea, loss of appetite, the painful cramps characteristic of IBS in some people, diarrhoea and heartburn. Ulcers are now known to be linked to infection with the *H. pylori* bacterium but there is a theory that stress helps it take hold.

The 'autonomic nervous system' controls processes such as digestion, over which we have no conscious control. The links between the brain and the digestion are very close and your gut contains a complex system of nerve cells and ganglia which are continually sending signals between the brain and the digestive system. The stomach and intestines between them have more nerve cells than the entire spinal cord. Of the body's entire production of serotonin, a chemical which helps to control mood, 95 per cent is found in the digestive system.

'The working gut is extremely complex and it is not surprising that things go wrong,' says Dr Bennett.

Processing the food you have eaten involves co-ordination of muscular contractions at the right speed, at the same time secreting the right chemicals and absorbing the right nutrients.

Experiments have been done in laboratories to show how stress has an effect on the way the gut works. One experiment measured gut activity after the subjects had been given complex and difficult arithmetic to do. Another measured it after what is called 'dichotomous hearing' which involved sending different sounds into each headphone, which again is very stressful for the subjects. Changes in the way the gut contracted and the secretions it produced could be measured by researchers.

The message from gastroenterologists is: listen to what your churning stomach is telling you and RELAX.

Learning to relax

True relaxation does not come easily to most of us. It's pretty much recognized that we all need to slow down and stop racing through life at 90 miles an hour. We grab a takeaway coffee and Danish on the run instead of enjoying a healthy breakfast. We gobble a sandwich in our minimal lunch break or starve all day before indulging in a takeaway in the evening. We try to juggle jobs, caring for the family, worry about elderly relatives, keeping husbands and partners happy, washing, ironing, cooking, cleaning, squeezing in time for hobbies, holidays and friends, keeping up with fashion, celebrity gossip and the state of the world – no wonder many of us are stressed!

It is really important, and not just for people with poor digestive health, to set aside some time in your busy schedule for relaxation. Even the most hard-pressed businesswoman needs to switch off from time to time, and even the most devoted mum needs 'me time'. Relaxation means different things to different people. You really need to give it a good deal of thought before deciding what would help you to relax. Some people find that a really tough gym work-out is the best way to forget a day slaving over a hot computer screen, but that doesn't work for everyone. Taking a holiday is often suggested as the best way to 'get away from it all'. Again, that isn't always the best way for everyone. If you are terrified of flying, or you are stuck for hours at a strike-bound airport with three wailing children, or you have had the kind of holiday where you share a villa with friends but you end up doing all the housework, you can end up more frazzled than when you went away!

If you suspect that stress may be at the root of your digestive problems and your GP agrees, you need to take a long, cool look at your life and see how you can reduce unnecessary stress and cope better with the stress that's left. We all have difficult situations to deal with and sadly, sometimes there are no easy answers. If you are in an especially stressful situation – facing up to a family bereavement, for instance, a divorce or separation, redundancy, a major life change like starting a new job, a house move, starting a family or the kids leaving home, you can expect to find it all stressful. In those circumstances, all you can do is be good to yourself, accept the help of friends, family and professionals if necessary, and ride out the storm. Even the blackest times don't last for ever. What you can also do is avoid piling stress on stress. If it's at all possible, don't try and tackle too many life changes at once – retirement and moving house, for example.

Perhaps, though, you aren't going through a major trauma but you still feel that life is just too much and you are only just keeping your head above water. You'll need to be honest with yourself about where the problems lie. If you have a difficult job, boss or colleagues, is there someone at work – a Union representative or human resources manager who could help you sort things out? Is it time to look for another job? Or even re-train for a different career? The fact that you are taking positive steps to make changes may reduce your feelings of stress.

Maybe it's your relationship that's causing you problems.

Communication is the answer here. Talking things over – without a row! – or perhaps booking a session with a Relate counsellor could help you to get things straight in your mind. There are always people out there who can offer a listening ear when you're finding life difficult – as well as friends and family there are the Samaritans, Parentline Plus if your youngsters are driving you mad, or organizations such as Age Concern and Help the Aged if you are worried about older members of the family. There are also support groups for people with serious illnesses and their carers. You are not alone.

It might seem a long way between worrying about your grumpy old Dad who really can't cope on his own but refuses all help, to your sore stomach or irritable bowel, but as we have already seen, the mind and the gut are very closely related. Whatever your problem, incorporating more relaxation in your life can only make things better.

Relaxation day to day

There are all sorts of little things you can do to switch off for five or ten minutes as part of your daily routine. In these days of mobile phones and BlackBerries, we are getting used to the idea we should always be available, but this just isn't true. Neither your office nor your family will fall apart if you take time out – so make sure you do. Here are some favourite stress-busting tips.

- Get up an hour earlier (this is one for larks!). Once you're used to it, 6 a.m. doesn't feel any different from 7 a.m., but it avoids an early-morning scrum at home, roads and trains are quieter and it enables you to have a productive half-hour in your office before the rest of your colleagues get in. If you're lucky, you might be able to negotiate flexible working hours with your boss.
- Incorporate some greenery into your daily life. It has been

proved that walking under trees reduces blood pressure. Could you arrange to walk to work through a park or along a riverbank? Could you spend lunchtime in the park too? Could you arrange your desk so that you have a leafy view to look out on? Bring some house plants to the office or create a roof garden? Put your name down for an allotment?

- Take up a really absorbing hobby. Men tend to be better at this than women, hence the number of golf or football widows! Singing in a choir, acting in a local drama group or rooting about at car-boot sales for 'collectables' can help you forget your troubles.
- Have a bath by candle-light.
- Send the children to stay with Granny or their best friend and spend a weekend in bed with your partner, just like you used to in the old days.
- Give yourself a spa treatment or other treat at home.
- Get your partner or a friend to give you a massage, or treat yourself to one at a local salon.
- Switch off the television for a week and get lost in a favourite book – see what your local library has to offer.
- Tune in to a different radio station from usual – Classic FM if you're a pop fan, Radio Two if you normally listen to Radio Four.
- We have already explored the beneficial effects of exercise in Chapter 5, but swimming, dance and gentle exercise like Pilates are especially recommended for relaxation.
- Contact with the natural world is proven to have a therapeutic effect. We can all learn about relaxation by watching a sleeping cat, and having to walk the dog can help you to appreciate green spaces, as suggested above. Dentists often have tanks of tropical fish in their surgeries to calm patients' nerves. If you haven't time to care for an animal, why not sponsor one you can visit at a zoo or rescue sanctuary?
- Laugh! Dr Robert Holden, who set up the first NHS Laughter

Clinic in the UK, recommends what he calls 'Transcendental Chuckling' which involves sitting in front of a mirror and laughing for two minutes for no reason whatsoever. Why not try it?

- Make sure you are eating a healthy diet. Stressed people use up a lot of vitamin C and also the B group vitamins, especially B5, B6 and B12. Unless you know they upset your digestion, eat plenty of wholegrain foods, fortified breakfast cereals, meat and fish or nuts and seeds, as well as your five-a-day of fruit and veg.
- Retain a sense of perspective. Many of the everyday problems that wind us up are not really that important, are they? When you find yourself getting stressed by a traffic jam or a long queue in the post office, just drop your shoulders, take a couple of deep, steady breaths, and repeat a soothing word or phrase to yourself, like 'calm' or 'peace' or 'All is well'.
- Create your own 'happy place'. There must be somewhere, sometime, some situation where you felt, or feel, completely at ease with yourself. Maybe on a favourite holiday beach, in a comfortable chair by the fire, or even in bed. Close your eyes for five minutes and take yourself there. See it in your mind's eye. Smell the tangy scent of the sea, of pine woods, of woodsmoke. Feel the grass or fine sand beneath your body, the warm rug over your knees, your cat's soft fur, your lover's arms round you. Listen to the sound of the waves, the crackle of the burning logs. Taste the coolness of a refreshing drink or the warmth of a soothing cuppa. Don't you feel better when you open your eyes again?

Help with relaxation

If you feel that simple, everyday moments of relaxation aren't enough to calm you down, there is plenty of help available. Some people find tranquillizing drugs helpful but these days they are usually only prescribed for short periods and for emergencies. There are also calming herbal and homoeopathic alternatives which don't have the side effects of pharmaceutical drugs. See Chapter 11 for more information on complementary medicines.

There are several forms of therapy which are especially recommended for relaxation, among them yoga, t'ai chi, qi gong, autogenic training and meditation of various kinds. Music, art and creativity generally are useful ways of de-stressing, either formally, by attending classes, or informally by 'writing out' all your worries in your diary. Many of us did that as teenagers and it works just as well for adults! There are also relaxation CDs and DVDs available commercially which can guide you through relaxation exercises, which you can then put into practice by yourself. If you find one of these that suits you, it can be really therapeutic. Let's look at each of these 'relaxation aids' in turn and consider what they might have to offer.

Yoga

The origins of yoga are lost in the mists of time but it may have started as much as 5,000 years ago. The word 'yoga' is derived from a Sanskrit word meaning 'union' and the idea of yoga is to bring about a perfect balance between mind and body by means of exercise, correct breathing and meditation. As well as having a relaxing effect, it is known that digestive disorders like heartburn, ulcers and IBS respond well to yoga. It is not competitive and you are not required to be a contortionist.

Yoga became popular in Britain in Victorian times but has really taken off since the 1960s. Although it is possible to learn yoga from a book or DVD, the most effective way to learn is almost certainly to take part in a class. Classes at all levels are widely available in most parts of the country. The British Wheel of Yoga (contact details on p. 114) can give you information about classes in your area.

T'ai chi

Chinese folklore states that t'ai chi was devised in the twelfth century by a Taoist monk. It is a combination of non-combative martial arts with breathing exercises and meditation. It is common in China to see groups of people, young and old, in city parks every morning, doing their graceful and unhurried t'ai chi exercises.

Like most Chinese therapies it is based on the idea that everything on Earth is controlled by two opposing elements, Yin and Yang, and that good physical and mental health requires that the two be brought into balance. Slow, fluid movements are designed to promote calm and harmony of mind and body. It is sometimes referred to as 'meditation in motion' which is a neat description. T'ai chi is particularly recommended for any stress-related disorder.

Qi gong

Like t'ai chi, qi gong is an Oriental therapy aimed at improving the flow of 'life energy' or qi within the body. A combination of gentle exercise, special breathing techniques, meditation and visualization is used. As in t'ai chi, the emphasis is on balance and harmony in both body and mind.

Autogenic training

A simple, effective technique for reducing stress, autogenic training (AT) is less well known than it should be, especially as it has been proven to work in a series of scientific studies. AT was invented almost 100 years ago by a German doctor, Johannes Schulz. He devised a series of simple mental exercises which bring about a profoundly relaxed state and help to switch off the body's stress response. Sleep disorders, indigestion and IBS can all be helped by a course of AT. It is available on the NHS at the country's five homoeopathic hospitals and can also be studied privately. A series of eight to ten sessions is usually enough to learn the exercises, which can then be practised at home as often as needed.

The British Autogenic Society (contact details on p. 114) can give you more details.

Meditation

There are many forms of meditation, coming from different cultural traditions and involving slightly different techniques. What they all have in common is that they help to calm you down and make you feel good. Scientifically speaking, meditation seems to shift brain activity to a different part of the brain – from the stress-prone right frontal cortex to the calmer left frontal cortex.

Meditation can be very simple, involving sitting or lying comfortably, relaxing all your muscles in turn, counting your breaths in and out, and focusing your mind on a single object such as a flower or a candle flame, a sound such as 'Om', or on visualizing a beautiful scene. Of course there is much more to learn if you wish to and an Internet search for 'meditation' can offer you many different choices.

8

Could it be an allergy?

It is fashionable, these days, to blame all sorts of health problems, including digestive difficulties, on an 'allergy'. If you have ever tried to cater for a dinner party which included vegetarians, vegans, and people who couldn't eat wheat-based foods or anything with milk in, you could be forgiven for wondering what is happening to us all. Older people can remember the days when everyone was expected to eat what was put in front of them and be grateful.

There is no doubt that allergies are on the increase, particularly among children. Allergic conditions like asthma, eczema, hay fever and so on have increased in incidence in the last 30 or 40 years and no one seems to know why. A report by the House of Lords Science and Technology Committee, published in September 2007, said that about a third of the population can expect to develop some sort of allergy during the course of their lives. The NHS has too few allergy specialists. Peanut allergy, once quite rare, is now said to affect as many as 1 in 50 children, and can lead to the most serious form of allergic reaction, anaphylactic shock.

Food allergy, however, is a tremendously complicated subject with a lot of disagreement even among the medical establishment, as well as among complementary and alternative practitioners. It's hard to obtain accurate figures for the numbers of people affected by unpleasant reactions to food. The British Nutrition Foundation claims that only about 1 to 2 per cent of the population suffer from 'food intolerance' and of these, only a relatively small proportion are truly allergic to food items.

In contrast, the campaigning charity Allergy UK (contact details on p. 114) believes that as many as 45 per cent of us have some form of 'food intolerance' which may cause digestive symptoms as well as other problems like migraine. Allergy UK produced a 'Stolen Lives' report in January 2007 after surveying 5,200 people with food problems. Many of these people did not feel that they were getting the right help from health professionals, even though in many cases their symptoms were seriously affecting their lives. Almost one in five – that is, 19.7 per cent of them – reported that they experienced digestive symptoms after eating certain foods. Symptoms included bloating, diarrhoea, vomiting and indigestion. Two-thirds said their GP 'did not understand' and the same proportion were not being treated by an allergy specialist or dietitian.

Allergy UK point out that it is people like these, for whom conventional medicine doesn't seem to have anything to offer, who are most at risk of trying out unproven 'alternative' methods of diagnosis and treatment. Everyone needs to eat a balanced diet, containing foods from all food groups – proteins, carbohydrates, fats, vitamins, minerals, fruit and vegetables – and those who have difficulty tolerating common foods need to find something equally nutritious to replace the things they can't eat.

The fact is that true 'food allergy' as doctors understand the term, is rarer than the general public thinks. This is because an 'allergy' is a particular response to a food item (or, of course, to another substance such as pollen).

What is an allergy?

An allergic reaction to a food happens when the body's immune system responds inappropriately to a substance (in this case a particular food) which, in normal healthy people, should not cause any adverse effects. The immune system is there to protect the body against 'invaders' in the form of foreign substances it perceives as a threat, such as bacteria and viruses. The immune system then produces antibodies known as immunoglobulin E, which can lead to the symptoms we recognize as an allergic reaction – not only redness and swelling of the skin and breathing difficulties but also stomach cramps, diarrhoea and vomiting. Food allergies of this type are known as IgE-mediated allergies, and are less common than other unpleasant reactions to specific foods or ingredients which do not involve IgE antibodies. This second type of reaction is not, strictly speaking, an allergy and is better described as food intolerance.

The most reliable forms of allergy testing are 'skin-prick testing' and blood tests, otherwise known as RAST (radioallergosorbant) tests, which are designed to measure the amount of IgE antibodies produced in response to a particular allergen. Skin-prick testing can be done in your GP's surgery by specially trained doctors or nurses. It involves placing a tiny drop of commercially produced allergen on to the skin, which is then pricked with a lancet. If you are truly allergic to the substance, whether milk or strawberries, your skin will start to itch and a small raised weal will appear within about 15 minutes. To be certain of the diagnosis, positive and negative controls are included. A drop of salt water, to which no reaction is expected, and a solution of histamine, to which everyone should react, are used as comparisons.

RAST tests are straightforward blood tests, done at your GP's surgery or in a hospital clinic. The blood sample is sent away with results available in a couple of weeks. Other forms of allergy testing, for example hair analysis and kinesiology, which measures muscle strength before and after exposure to an allergen, are often advertised. However, a major report on allergy produced by the Royal College of Physicians in 2003 found no independent evidence that these tests were accurate or effective. Allergy testing is sometimes offered on a 'walk-in' basis in pharmacies, but although the blood tests offered may prove accurate, the results really need to be interpreted by a doctor. If you are seriously affected by a food allergy you will need a properly worked-out diet, so it's best to ask your GP to refer you to a dietitian or allergy specialist.

What is food intolerance?

The British Nutrition Foundation (contact details on p. 114) defines food intolerance as 'a non-psychological, reproducible, unpleasant reaction to a specific food or ingredient'. Simply disliking or avoiding a food is not food intolerance. If you can't tolerate, for example, tomatoes or shellfish, it means that the same uncomfortable symptoms recur every time you eat those items. Food intolerance is not the same as food poisoning, either. This is most commonly caused by eating food that has gone 'off' or been infected by common bacteria such as salmonella or *E. coli* (See Chapter 3).

In recent years, more and more stories have appeared in the press about wheat intolerance, and this has led to more people wondering whether cutting out wheat from their diets might improve symptoms like bloating or those associated with IBS. The British Nutrition Foundation reports that there is no evidence that wheat intolerance is really on the increase and points out that, as wheat is an important and nutritious staple in the British diet, avoiding it can make healthy eating really difficult. Wheat is not only a major ingredient in obvious food items like bread, cakes, pasta and breakfast cereals, but is also used as a thickening agent in a huge range of other foods like sauces and soups and to bulk up items such as sausages and pâté. Beer also contains a detectable level of a protein present in wheat. Avoiding wheat altogether is not only difficult and problematic socially, but it also removes good sources of vitamins and minerals in the diet, since wheat flour has to be fortified with iron and B vitamins by law. Wheat products like wholemeal bread, cakes and pasta are also high in fibre, so contribute to a healthy diet in other ways too.

The commonest form of wheat intolerance is coeliac disease (described on p. 28), a condition in which the protein gluten, found in wheat, rye, barley and possibly in oats, damages the lining of the gut. This leads to pain and difficulty in absorbing the valuable nutrients in food, such as iron, calcium and fat. Coeliac disease is diagnosed by a blood test and coeliacs find that their health improves once they are able to follow a strict gluten-free diet.

True allergy to wheat – involving IgE antibodies – is thought to be very rare. Some people, however, find that, although they are not allergic to wheat and tests for coeliac disease come up negative, eating a lot of wheat-based products such as bread and pasta leads to bloating and stomach discomfort. As with all food intolerance, the only way to discover whether wheat is the true cause of these digestive problems is to cut it out of your diet for an experimental period. We shall be looking at 'exclusion diets' later in this chapter. It is worth saying at this point that if you are thinking of embarking on a true exclusion diet, as opposed to avoiding wheat for a short time, you really need to do this under the supervision of an expert, either your GP, or a dietitian or nutritionist. The Sussex-based Natural Health Advisory Service/Women's Nutrition Clinic (contact details on p. 115) also has considerable experience of exclusion diets of all kinds. You might also find it helpful to contact an organization called Foods Matter (contact details on p. 115) which produces a monthly magazine with helpful information on food intolerance, including specially adapted recipes.

Diagnosing food intolerance

A blood test for food intolerance called the 'York Test' is available by post and has been recommended in recent years by Allergy UK. A double-blind, randomly controlled clinical trial of 150 people with irritable bowel syndrome found that this test, which is intended to identify food intolerances and place subjects on an appropriate diet, could be effective. For more information about the York Test, see p. 116.

Food intolerance can be difficult to diagnose because no two people's symptoms are exactly the same and, as we have seen, bloating, nausea, indigestion and bowel problems can be caused by so many different things. You might consider food intolerance as a cause of your digestive problems after your GP has ruled out other possible causes, or you might have been diagnosed with IBS and realized that your symptoms worsen when you eat a particular food.

People can be sensitive to almost any kind of food, from staples like wheat and dairy products which are difficult to avoid, to items like shellfish or more unusual fruits which can be cut out of the diet without too many problems. Lactose intolerance – the condition in which the body does not produce enough of the enzyme lactase to digest milk products properly can cause stomach discomfort and bloating. Try replacing dairy with soya products. Many people find that occasional food items 'disagree with them' and if mushrooms make you ill, beans give you wind, or onions 'repeat' on you, don't eat them. For some people, it isn't that simple. It may be the additives in much of today's processed food that cause problems. Look at the list of chemicals listed in common supermarket-bought foods or ready-meals and you can be forgiven for wondering why we need sulphites, benzoates, salicylates, monosodium glutamate, aspartame and tartrazine in our food. All of these can cause reactions in some people.

If you suspect that food intolerance could be at the root of your digestive problems, the best way to discover the culprit is by keeping a 'food diary' for a time. Annoyingly, food intolerance comes and goes. Some people find that their digestion never seems to have recovered after a bad bout of gastroenteritis which has left them sensitive to foods they could originally eat without problems. Others find that avoiding a food item for a time clears the problem up and they can ultimately re-introduce it without difficulty.

Another reason why diagnosing food intolerance is difficult is that symptoms don't appear immediately. This makes the condition very different from classic allergy, where symptoms can appear within moments of eating the suspect food. Keeping a food diary can help, but may not offer all the answers. You'll need to keep a record of all your symptoms as well as a careful note of everything you eat and see whether some sort of pattern begins to emerge.

The best way to obtain a true diagnosis of food intolerance is to exclude a suspect food from your diet for a time. If your symptoms improve or disappear, it's 'problem solved' – especially if they recur when you start eating the offending food item again. However, few cases are that simple as many people find that several different foods, or a combination of foods, cause their difficulties. This is one reason why experts recommend that you only undertake a true 'exclusion diet' with proper medical supervision. The other, of course, is that cutting too many staple and nutritious foods from your diet can, if taken to extremes, leave you seriously malnourished.

Having said that, if your food-symptom diary has led you to believe that wheat products, dairy or eggs might cause your digestive problems, it is much easier than it used to be to find acceptable substitutes. Nearly all the major supermarkets now carry 'free from' ranges of popular foods. Customer services departments can often tell you more about exactly which of their products are suitable for you. You can buy, for example, wheat-free pasta, cakes, biscuits and breakfast cereals, so you don't need to starve. Health-food stores and speciality grocers also sell wheat- and dairy-free products, although they tend to be expensive. You can replace dairy milk with soya milk – some brands being fortified with extra calcium – and there are many soya-based desserts and yoghurts.

Bread can be more of a problem. Wheat-free bread is available but it tends to have a heavy texture making it seem indigestible. Some wheat-free breads are acceptable toasted or in the form of pitta bread. The only way to find one that suits your digestion is to experiment. People with known or suspected food intolerances get used to reading the labels on pre-packaged or processed foods, familiarizing themselves with the terms used in food labelling, and identifying items like sodium caseinate, whey and lactose if they can't tolerate dairy products, since all these items are derived from milk.

There are several magazines aimed at the health-conscious which carry pages of advertisements from companies producing dairy-free, gluten-free and egg-free foods. Many offer recipe booklets as well. A browse round the cookery section of your local library or bookshop should also yield plenty of books catering for special diets and telling you how to adapt favourite recipes for those unable to tolerate certain foods. Vegetarian and vegan societies are also good sources of help.

Adopting an exclusion diet

It is possible to be affected by almost any food, but those least likely to cause problems include

- meats: lamb, chicken
- vegetables: rice, sweet potato, carrots, asparagus, rhubarb
- fruit: (peeled) pear, banana, apricot, apple, pineapple
- fats: non-dairy margarine, sunflower oil, olive oil
- others: herb or Rooibos tea (available from health stores), honey, sugar, sago.

What might be described as 'do-it-yourself diagnosis', achieved by keeping a food/symptom diary and trying to manage without wheat or dairy products for a week or two might not offer the solutions you hope for. Food intolerance is a complex area, even for experts. For one thing, many people actually crave the food that upsets them and suffer from withdrawal symptoms when they cut it out. A sudden and complete change from your usual diet might upset a delicate and stressed digestion in any case. These are all reasons why it's a good idea, if adopting a strict exclusion diet, to do this under supervision.

'When someone comes to me asking about food intolerance, the first thing I do is take a look at their current diet,' says registered dietitian Emma Mills.

If they are missing meals or eating a lot of processed foods, that in itself could be causing problems.

Most people who suspect food intolerance come to me after they have tried manipulating their diet to some extent already, which is fine. What I advise is that they keep a symptom chart and carefully note down all their symptoms on a scale of 1 to 10, everything from bloating and constipation to headaches. Then I might suggest that they exclude foods that seem to upset them and evaluate their symptoms again after a two-week 'wash-out'. Then we try re-introducing the suspect foods, one at a time, and seeing whether the symptoms recur.

If a certain food seems to trigger severe symptoms when it is re-introduced, then that is the diagnosis and I help them to adopt a nutritionally balanced diet which excludes the problem foods. The more basic the food, the more careful you have to be. For example, a gluten-free diet can be short on fibre and a dairy-free diet might be lacking in calcium, which has particular implications for women who may be at risk of osteoporosis.

I would not recommend being on an exclusion diet for any length of time, or staying on it if it doesn't make any difference to your symptoms, because of the risk of missing out on essential nutrients. Those who do have to manage food intolerance might find it easier if they are home cooks rather than eating a lot of pre-packaged, processed or ready meals which rely on ingredients or additives which many people can't tolerate.

When you are re-introducing a suspect food, you need to do it carefully. Don't, for example, drink a whole glass of milk on an empty stomach. It's better to serve a portion of cauliflower cheese and see what kind of effect that has. An exclusion diet works best if followed in a measured and systematic way so that you can identify the problem food accurately and don't exclude any more nutrients than strictly necessary.

If you do have to avoid wheat there are alternatives like rice and corn flakes, but you may have to focus on alternative sources of fibre, such as fruit and vegetables. Wheat-based products like granary bread, wholewheat cereals and muesli are generally good for the digestion because they provide plenty of fibre. An ideal diet has as much variety as possible and if you are planning to exclude two major food groups, such as wheat and dairy, you may miss out on a range of nutrients such as B vitamins and iodine. I would always advise making these up from the diet but if that isn't possible, supplements may be required.

Emma believes that there should be more research into food intolerance and that it shouldn't be dismissed by health professionals, as is still sometimes the case. She recommends fresh, natural, home-cooked meals featuring as wide a variety of foods as possible.

'You are less likely to develop a food intolerance if you eat well,' she comments. 'Eating healthily – no skipping breakfast, the minimum of processed food – means that your gut will be well nourished and that will help it to do its job properly.'

9

What your GP can do

Most of us are reluctant to take what we think of as ordinary, everyday 'tummy troubles' to our GP. This is perfectly understandable. For one thing, the vast majority of mild stomach upsets, aches and pains, or temporary bouts of constipation or diarrhoea, either clear up by themselves or with the help of home remedies or preparations you can buy over the counter. A better diet, with plenty of fruit and vegetables, making sure you drink abundant plain water, giving up smoking, going easy on alcohol, exercising and a generally healthier lifestyle can protect your digestive system against some of the difficulties it might encounter – even if you have a weakness for hot curries, or decide to go backpacking in the Amazon jungle!

There is another reason why we are reluctant to go to the GP with digestive problems though, and that is embarrassment. Many of the gastroenterology specialists I spoke to for this book mentioned the 'blush factor' when considering why digestive troubles, which are so common, don't hit the headlines very often.

'People are happy to discuss their heart attacks but bowels are just not something they are willing to talk about on the whole,' said one consultant. Another said that men, in particular, are often extremely bashful about admitting there is something wrong with their digestion. That's one up for women, because if you do have a serious bowel condition it's much better to find out sooner, rather than later. Bowel cancer, for example, is curable if found before it has spread beyond the inner lining of the bowel. Don't let shyness or embarrassment prevent you from obtaining a diagnosis and treatment that could very well save your life.

As the charity Bowel Cancer UK says, bowels are the body's natural waste system, like the kitchen wastebin at home. GPs, nurses and gastroenterology specialists are perfectly comfortable discussing these parts of the body and their functions. Your GP will have heard it all before, so don't let embarrassment hold you back.

London GP Dr Sarah Jarvis comments:

> I see patients with digestive problems several times a week. Many women come in with a 'hidden agenda' and will talk about something else at first, only mentioning their bowel problem at the end of the consultation. If you find it difficult to talk about, you could try practising what you want to say with your partner or a friend or in front of a mirror before you go to the doctor, or writing down the questions you want to ask. If you need more time, ask the surgery for a 20-minute appointment, and if you'd feel happier seeing a female doctor, then ask to see one.

Anyone who has ever had a baby knows that in the first days and weeks after the birth you examine the contents of the little one's nappy carefully to make sure all is as it should be. As an adult, the message for digestive health should be – know your poo! Just a glance into the toilet bowl before you flush is enough for you to check that all is well. What you should be looking out for is a change in the look of your stools, especially when combined with a change in the frequency of your visits to the loo. Problems that should be checked out by your GP have already been listed in Chapter 4 but are worth repeating here:

- any bleeding from the bottom unaccompanied by straining, itching or soreness;
- a persistent change of bowel habit, for example needing to go to the toilet more often or having looser stools;
- severe abdominal pain before or after eating;

- persistent feelings of fullness, bloating, indigestion, heartburn, nausea or vomiting;
- unexpected loss of appetite or weight loss when not dieting;
- tiredness and lethargy accompanied by abdominal symptoms such as those listed above.

Remember that many of these symptoms can be caused by non-serious and easily curable conditions. All the same, they are definitely worth checking out.

How you can help your doctor

In order to help you, your GP will need to know as much as possible about your symptoms when you go to the surgery. For example,

- If you have 'stomach' pain, exactly where is it – above your waist or lower down? On the right or the left side? Is it a dull, dragging pain, a sharp cramping pain, or a griping pain? Is it a constant ache or does it come and go?
- Does any pain occur before or after meals?
- Do you feel sick, or have you been sick?
- Have you noticed any change in your bowel movements – are you constipated, do you have diarrhoea, or a mixture of both, are you passing any blood or mucus?

Your GP will probably also ask you some questions about your diet and lifestyle, including how much alcohol you are drinking, and whether you have tried any over-the-counter medication. It can help to keep a 'symptom diary' so that you don't forget anything which might be significant.

Finding out what's wrong

Dr Sarah Jarvis says that the tests your GP gives you are tests of exclusion. This means that they are given in order to exclude the possibility of serious disease, such as cancer, or to find out whether your condition requires further investigation. You will be given blood tests, to find out whether you are anaemic – which could indicate that further investigation is necessary – and whether your liver is working properly. You will be offered advice on healthy eating and other lifestyle changes, including relaxation therapies such as hypnotherapy, as stress is such a common cause of digestive problems. An OTC medicine such as Gaviscon may be suggested. Alternatively, your GP may prescribe one of the highly successful drugs now available for ulcers, such as ranitidine – from a class of drugs called H2 receptor antagonists – or omeprazole or lansoprazole – from a class of drugs called proton-pump inhibitors. All these drugs work by reducing the amount of acid in the stomach, allowing ulcers and the discomfort of gastritis time to heal.

'If the medication your GP prescribes does not seem to help, or you find it upsets your stomach, go back to the surgery and let your doctor know,' Dr Jarvis advises. 'There are several suitable drugs and if one doesn't agree with you, ask if you can try another.'

If the treatment your GP prescribes does not seem to be solving the problem, she will probably refer you to your local hospital for further tests aiming to find out what is really wrong. The most common tests for digestive problems include endoscopy, colonoscopy/sigmoidoscopy, ultrasound and barium swallow/meal/enema. All these tests are basically different ways of allowing medical staff to have a good look at your digestive system and the way it is working – or not working. They usually involve an outpatient visit to the gastroenterology department of the local hospital.

Endoscopy

An endoscope is a long, flexible tube incorporating a tiny camera and a light. You need to swallow this so that the doctors can see the inside of your oesophagus, stomach and duodenum and make sure that everything looks normal and that there are no growths or sore-looking areas which could be ulcers forming. If there is anything suspicious, the doctor will take a small tissue sample – a biopsy – which will be sent for analysis.

The tube and camera are very tiny so that it is possible to have this test without sedation. Alternatively, you can have a sedative which will make you really drowsy, or a light anaesthetic, in which case you feel nothing at all. Sometimes you can choose which you are given. If you are very nervous, tell the doctors. They may also spray the back of your throat to numb it and make it easier to pass the tube down.

Your GP or the hospital should give you instructions, or may send you a leaflet with your appointment letter, to tell you about the test and about what you should do to prepare for it. You will be asked not to have anything to eat or drink for some hours beforehand so that your stomach is empty. If you are planning to have a sedative or anaesthetic, you will need someone to go home with you afterwards to make sure you're all right. Your stomach may feel a little bloated or your throat may be sore, or you may feel perfectly all right.

Procedures may vary slightly between hospitals. You may be told the results of the endoscopy straight away, or the results may be sent to your GP in a couple of weeks.

Colonoscopy or sigmoidoscopy

These are similar tests to an endoscopy but starting at the other end of your digestive system, if you have been having problems with your bowel and/or pains in the lower part of your digestive tract. These tests are usually performed under sedation, during which a flexible tube is passed through your back passage and up into your bowel. A sigmoidoscopy looks at the part of the bowel known as the sigmoid colon, which is where most cases of bowel cancer occur. A colonoscopy enables the doctor to look for any abnormalities over the whole length of the bowel. As well as bowel cancer, a colonoscopy can also reveal any inflammation of the area, or polyps, which are small non-cancerous growths on the bowel wall.

Preparation for a colonoscopy is a bit more complicated than for an endoscopy. Your doctor or the hospital will let you know what you have to do to prepare for this test. Your bowel needs to be empty so that the doctor can see the bowel wall clearly, so you will have to go on a liquids-only diet for a short time, drink plenty of clear fluid on the day before the colonoscopy, and also take a laxative. It is very important that you follow the instructions you are given.

During the test the colonoscope is inserted gently into the colon. Air is often pumped in to make it easier for the doctors to see what's happening. They will examine the pictures of your bowel on a small screen and if necessary, your doctor will remove any tissue for a biopsy or remove any existing polyps. A colonoscopy takes from 20 to 30 minutes and shouldn't be painful, though it can feel uncomfortable.

Again, you will need to rest and take things easy after the procedure, and you will be advised to have someone with you as you go home and for a few hours afterwards. Results may be given to you straight away or a few days later – ask the doctors about this so that you are sure when to expect them. If you still feel drowsy after sedation it can help if the doctor writes things down for you.

Ultrasound scan

An ultrasound scan is a painless test which uses high-frequency sound waves to create images of your body's organs. These can be studied by a specially trained technician who can recognize any abnormalities. For example, ultrasound can travel through liquid, but will bounce back, creating an 'echo', when it hits a solid surface. This means that when a probe is placed over the gall bladder, the ultrasound waves can travel through the bile it contains but will create an 'echo' if it hits a solid gall stone.

Ultrasound can be used to help diagnose problems in many of the digestive organs including the abdomen, liver, gall bladder and pancreas, since it is able to tell the difference between a harmless cyst, which may be full of fluid, and a solid tumour. If you are referred for ultrasound you may be asked not to eat for a certain number of hours beforehand. You have to lie on a couch while the operator moves the probe around the areas of your body to be scanned, so that she can 'see' your organs from different angles. It is not painful, though if the operator presses down hard it can be slightly uncomfortable, and there is no need for you to be sedated. The test can take between 15 and 45 minutes and results are available straight away.

As far as is known there are no side effects from ultrasound and you can go home as soon as the test is completed.

Barium swallow/meal/enema

With newer techniques like endoscopy and colonoscopy becoming more and more sophisticated, barium treatments are not used as often as they used to be. A barium treatment is a kind of X-ray, but because the digestive tract doesn't show up very well on ordinary X-rays, patients are asked to drink a liquid containing barium sulphate, which does show up clearly on X-ray pictures. If you are given a barium enema, a small tube is placed in your back passage and the barium liquid is then passed into your colon.

Again, the idea is for the doctors to be able to see what is going on in the different areas of your digestive tract. During a barium swallow, it is your oesophagus which is looked at and you normally stand in front of the X-ray machine. A barium meal is used to diagnose any problems in your stomach and duodenum and takes a little longer. If your doctors think there may be a problem in your small intestine, you may have to wait until the barium has passed into this area before the X-ray pictures are taken. The doctors or hospital should give you information about preparing for these tests as you have to go without food for several hours beforehand.

As with a barium meal, a barium enema involves lying on a couch while X-rays are taken, this time of your lower bowel. You will have been given laxatives and advice about how long to go without food beforehand. You may have to change position so that all areas of your colon can be seen clearly.

You will be able to go home soon after these treatments are finished. You may feel nauseous and the barium may make you constipated and turn your stools very pale but side effects are rare.

An important point – if you have diabetes, you should make sure that anyone giving you any of these tests knows, so that you do not have to go without food for any longer than necessary. Tests involving X-rays should not be given to pregnant women.

Rosemary, 46, went to her GP with severe indigestion and was given a full range of tests.

At first they thought I had an ulcer but the blood test for helicobacter came back negative. I was still given 'triple therapy' drugs for a couple of weeks but they didn't seem to make any difference. I was then referred for endoscopy. I am totally unused to hospitals and medical treatments so I was very nervous but it really was nothing to worry about. I was given a light general anaesthetic and was 'out' for about an hour according to the friend who came with me. I was given written information as soon as I came round, saying that they had found only 'mild gastritis' or inflammation of the stomach lining. This was reassuring but didn't stop the pain.

I also had ultrasound which was a bit uncomfortable but revealed nothing abnormal. I was sent for a barium swallow, but was told that as I'd already had an endoscopy there was no point. Eventually the consultant I saw said my tummy problems were probably the result of stress so I took up relaxation therapies, which do help a bit, backed up by ranitidine tablets if I need them.

Drug treatments

After a barrage of tests, either in your GP's surgery or your local gastroenterology department, you should have a much better idea of what is going wrong, if not a definite diagnosis. According to CORE, the majority of patients who attend gastroenterology clinics have what are known as 'functional disorders' such as irritable bowel syndrome, rather than any organic disease. Your GP may very well prescribe the sort of lifestyle changes we have already looked at in the chapters on diet, exercise, stress management and avoiding the enemies of good digestive health.

10

If you need an operation ...

The chances are that your digestive problems can be treated without the need for surgery. Drug treatments, both over the counter and prescription only, are improving all the time, and many conditions respond to this kind of care, plus a few lifestyle changes. As an example, 20 or 30 years ago, patients with stomach or duodenal ulcers faced just two choices. Either they combined an extremely boring diet with antacids, or they had to have surgery. However, the discovery that the bacterium *H. pylori* was implicated in ulcer problems, plus the development of not one, but two classes of drugs that were extremely effective in treating it, means that these days, people with ulcers only need operations when there are severe complications.

In most other cases, treatment is with 'H2 receptor antagonists' such as cimetidine and ranitidine, or 'proton-pump inhibitors' such as lansoprazole and omeprazole – sometimes in addition to antibiotics, the 'triple-therapy' approach.

With other conditions such as Crohn's disease and ulcerative colitis, surgery is offered as a last resort when other forms of treatment have proved ineffective. For some digestive problems, however, surgery is still the treatment of choice. For example, appendectomy – removal of the appendix – is a common and routine operation. Almost 45,000 appendectomies were carried out in the UK in 2006, a figure that has fallen by two-thirds in the last 40 years. In more serious conditions such as digestive cancers, surgery is one of the main forms of treatment, and is often combined with radiotherapy or chemotherapy. A diagnosis of cancer is often made after a 'biopsy' in which a surgeon removes a small amount of tissue. He then sends it off to the lab for tests which will confirm whether cancer is present. If this is the case, then further surgery takes place to remove the tumour and also nearby tissue where more cancer cells might be lurking. The extent of any cancer surgery will always depend on where exactly the cancer is and how far it has spread. Sometimes a tumour cannot be completely removed but symptoms can be relieved by removing part of it.

Don't be afraid to ask questions if you are told you need any kind of surgery. Your specialist will be glad to answer them. Sometimes you are offered a choice of treatments, which can be bewildering unless you happen to be an expert. This is where the patient-support groups, such as Cancerbackup (see p. 114) or the National Association for Colitis and Crohn's Disease (see p. 115), can be tremendously helpful. They have patient helplines you can call to obtain more information about the operation, so that you can become as well informed as possible and be helped to make the right decision in your individual circumstances.

Many operations these days – not only those on the digestive system – are done using a technique called laparoscopy or 'keyhole surgery'. As this involves smaller incisions, it is less of a shock to the system and recovery times are usually quicker, especially for normally fit and healthy patients.

What actually happens is that the surgeon looks at the organ to be removed using a telescope-type of instrument or instruments, called a 'laparoscope'. The patient is given a general anaesthetic and small incisions are made into which the laparoscope can be inserted. Then the surgeon can see what's going on on a TV screen and proceed from there. The abdomen is often inflated using carbon dioxide gas so that it's easier for the surgeon to see.

'Laparoscopic surgery has huge advantages for the patient,' says Dr John Bennett, Chairman of CORE.

With traditional surgery, a large incision is made in the abdomen. While it heals it can be painful for the patient to move, or even cough. With laparoscopic surgery, a number of tiny little nicks are made and many patients are able to leave hospital the next day. Operations which used to be difficult, such as surgery for hiatus hernias or reflux, are made simpler with the use of laparoscopy. Surgeons need special training and slightly different skills such as the ability to manipulate long instruments. As with any surgery, complications do occasionally occur and other organs can be damaged. It is also possible that your surgeon will begin using a laparoscope and find that open surgery is required after all. He should let you know in advance that this may happen.

Not all conditions are suitable for laparoscopic surgery. It is less often used when part of the large bowel is being removed because of cancer. It is also less common in treating appendicitis, pancreatitis or any condition where there is inflammation and danger of any infection spreading.

What we are also seeing in GI [gastrointestinal] surgery is increasing specialization. Fifty years ago, 'general surgeons' tackled all kinds of operations. Now, GI surgery is a speciality and within that there are surgeons who specialize in the different organs, such as the colon, pancreas or liver. Surgeons also work as part of a team. If you are being treated for cancer your surgeon will work together with an oncologist who makes the decisions about pre- and post-operative chemotherapy or radiotherapy.

What will you need to know?

Questions you might want to ask your surgeon or specialist could include:

- What does the operation actually involve?
- What sort of preparations do I need to make?
- How will the operation be carried out?
- How long will I be in hospital?
- What sort of after-effects can be expected?
- Will I be able to resume a normal life afterwards – including returning to work – and if so, how soon?
- If there anything I can do to cure myself?

- Is there any alternative to this operation?
- How high is the success rate of the operation?
- What are the possible complications?

Appendectomy

Having your appendix out is a routine operation and is a common emergency procedure although less common than it used to be. An 'open' operation involves an incision in the lower right-hand side of the abdomen through which the inflamed or infected appendix is removed. An appendectomy lasts between one and two hours and will mean a hospital stay of a few days. You'll be treated with antibiotics to prevent infection and also painkillers where needed.

Gall bladder removal

The technical name for this operation is cholecystectomy. These days it is usually done via 'keyhole surgery' or laparoscopy. A series of four small incisions enables the organ to be removed and the bile duct is clipped with small metal clips. If there is excessive bleeding or any other complications, 'open' surgery may have to be performed, through an incision in the abdomen. This leaves a bigger scar, which will fade in time. If all goes well, you will wake after the anaesthetic hooked up to a 'drip' for fluids but you will be able to eat and drink again within a few hours. You'll need to take painkillers while your wound heals but the stitches usually dissolve by themselves. After keyhole surgery you can usually bath or shower the next day. As with all surgery, you're encouraged to get up and walk about as soon as you are able, to avoid the possibility of blood clots. Depending on your job you could be back at work in two weeks.

Valerie was in her 40s when she began getting extremely severe stomach pains which effectively laid her low for days at a time.

I was in such pain that I tried the kind of breathing I'd learned when I was in labour! I have always had stomach problems because I was taking anti-inflammatories for arthritis and they didn't agree with me. I was then prescribed ranitidine and the doctors I saw told me to increase the dose because I had 'oesophageal spasms'.

This went on for some time and was really debilitating. Eventually I made such a fuss that my GP referred me to a different hospital consultant for a second opinion. He said straight away that it sounded like a gall bladder problem and advised me to cut down on fats in my diet, which helped. Four months later I went into hospital to have my gall bladder removed using keyhole surgery. They made four tiny cuts, I was in hospital for just three days and haven't had any trouble since.

I really should have been diagnosed sooner as I was middle-aged, a bit overweight and my mother had had the same operation years ago.

Surgery for severe acid reflux or GORD

This condition may be treated surgically if lifestyle changes and/ or drug treatments don't seem to be working. Laparoscopy is the usual technique used for this operation which goes by the impressive name of 'Nissen Fundoplication'. Five small incisions are made and the valve between the oesophagus and the stomach is reinforced by wrapping part of the upper stomach around the lower part of the oesophagus. The operation may require as little as one to three days in hospital and there are few long-term side effects. After the operation there should be no more need for medication and you should be able to resume normal activities in two to three weeks.

Hiatus hernias may require an operation, as a last resort, if they haven't responded to medication; your doctor will advise you if this is the case. Hiatus hernia surgery is a 'keyhole' operation which basically tightens up the 'hiatus' area, the gap in the diaphragm where the oesophagus fits. The operation keeps the stomach in its correct place, below the diaphragm, and involves perhaps three or four days in hospital followed by a week's recuperation. In the case of an ulcer, an operation will cut the nerves which control acid production, or even remove the acid-producing part of the stomach. An ulcer which perforates causes severe pain and collapse. This is a medical emergency for which immediate surgical repair is essential.

With any operation on the digestive system, it is sensible to ask advice about any possible changes of diet and eating habits afterwards. You will be on liquids only at first, then later you will be able to cope with things like soup and yoghurt, but you may well find that your tolerance for different foods has changed. It's only by trial and error that you can work out what agrees with your new, improved digestive system and what doesn't. This is especially true if you have a major operation, such as those for inflammatory bowel disease or cancer.

Surgery for cancers of the digestive tract

Surgery is a common form of treatment for cancers of the digestive tract. Usually, the tumour is removed from the affected organ together with some of the surrounding tissue, so that the surgeons can be as sure as possible that the area is free from all cancer cells. Obviously, this is major surgery and can be a daunting prospect but in many cases it is life-saving. The doctors and surgeons treating you will be pleased to answer your questions about just what is involved. Again, it is always worth consulting patients-support groups like Cancerbackup, who have specialist nurses on hand to offer advice and reassurance, as well as information leaflets.

An operation for oesophageal cancer will depend on the size and position of the tumour and how far it has spread. As the oesophagus is a long tube, the affected portion can be removed and the stomach joined to the shortened oesophagus which is left, meaning that after the operation your stomach will be higher up towards your chest. You may be nursed after the operation in intensive care or a high-dependency unit. Initially you will be on a drip for fluids plus a nasogastric tube and possibly chest drains. You will be prescribed painkillers and physiotherapy to help clear your lungs of fluid. As you begin to recover, you will be encouraged to move about to avoid the formation of blood clots. It's likely that you will lose weight and, as with all gastrointestinal surgery, you will have to pay special attention to your diet after the operation. Eating smaller meals more often and remembering to eat slowly can help – Cancerbackup has plenty of information about life after this type of surgery.

Surgery for stomach cancer has shown improving results in the last ten years. As with many cancers, your chances are much better if you are diagnosed early. The operation will involve removing the tumour and part of the surrounding stomach tissue. Post-operative care is similar to that for oesophageal cancer. You'll be able to take small sips of water after a couple of days and a light diet after four to five days, and will be encouraged to move around as soon as possible.

The medical staff treating you should give you advice about life after this type of surgery. It will take time to recover your full health and you may find that you want to eat less. Small, regular meals, eaten slowly, and including as wide a variety of foods as possible, are usually recommended.

Some patients suffer from a condition known as 'dumping syndrome' after this type of surgery. Either immediately after eating, or within a hour or two of a meal, they may feel dizzy or faint, or have palpitations. This is caused by a sudden drop in blood pressure. Some people find they are helped by eating small, regular meals which are low in sugar. Drinking and eating at separate times can also help.

If you have had surgery for cancer you should be regularly monitored afterwards to check on your progress so that any after effects can be dealt with. The total recovery period can be as long as six months. Your newly adapted digestive system might have trouble absorbing sufficient calcium or iron from your diet, in which case supplements will be prescribed for you.

Pancreatic cancer can also be treated with surgery, particularly if it is diagnosed in its early stages. Depending on the exact site of the tumour, it may be possible to remove part of the pancreas, or the whole of the organ, or the whole organ together with part of the stomach, small bowel and the gall bladder, a procedure known as a Whipple's operation. Post-operative care is similar to that for other cancer surgery. If your whole pancreas is removed you will need insulin injections to make up for the insulin your pancreas produced, as well as drugs containing the enzymes produced by your healthy pancreas.

Surgery for bowel cancer

If you are diagnosed with bowel cancer – cancer of the colon or rectum – surgery is one of the most common treatments. We've already seen that the bowel is a long tube; the surgeons will remove the cancer and join the two ends together. That makes it sound rather more simple than it is as there are cases where the two 'ends' of the bowel cannot be joined for some reason. In that case, the upper end is brought out on to the skin of the abdomen in what is called a 'stoma'. This is an opening through which the waste products (faeces) pass, to be collected in a specially designed bag or pouch. This is known as a colostomy. An ileostomy is effectively the same operation, involving a different part of the bowel.

In many cases of bowel cancer, the colostomy or ileostomy is only a temporary arrangement and another operation takes place several months later to join up the bowel again. If the tumour was located in the lower part of the bowel, the rectum, you are more likely to need a permanent colostomy.

As with many digestive operations, there is often a choice between open and keyhole surgery, but this will depend on exactly where the tumour is. Post-operative care follows a similar pattern as for other 'digestive' cancers and you will probably be in hospital for around ten days.

Surgery for inflammatory bowel disease and diverticular disease

If you have either Crohn's disease, ulcerative colitis or diverticular disease and your condition does not respond to drug treatment, you may need to have part of your bowel removed. The result is similar and you might also have to live with a colostomy, either on a temporary or permanent basis.

Living with a colostomy

You will probably feel that living with a colostomy is quite a daunting prospect, and it can be very reassuring to contact other people who have found that there is life after this type of operation. The Reading-based Colostomy Association (contact details on p. 115) produces helpful leaflets on dealing with every aspect of life with a colostomy, including advice on day-to-day management as well as tips on travel, clothing, diet and any possible complications.

The number of patients with stomas is actually declining because new ways of managing the conditions which lead to stomas are being introduced all the time. Appliances and products designed for the management of stoma care have also improved in recent years. If you have this kind of operation, you will be shown how to take care of your stoma by a specially trained stoma nurse.

You will need to care for your stoma properly because bowel contents can irritate the skin of the abdomen and there is also the possibility of an allergy to some of the materials used. You also need to manage your diet carefully as some foods will cause excess wind or possibly diarrhoea. Skin care, plus the practicalities of dealing with the bags used to collect faeces, will be explained to you by your stoma nurse.

It can be difficult at first to adjust psychologically to this way of life. You may not be prepared for the way your stoma looks, you might feel the whole thing is terrifying or repulsive and be afraid that something is going to go wrong and embarrassing leakage could occur. This is perfectly natural and something it can take time to come to terms with. You have to remember that thousands of people in this country are living with a stoma and still taking part in normal activities – ranging from active sports to love-making.

Jean has been a 'colostomate' for five years since her operation for bowel cancer.

The first shock was being told I had cancer, and that overshadowed the fact that I had a colostomy. I told myself that it was saving my life. I've since met people who lived for years with colitis or diverticular disease and couldn't go anywhere because they were afraid to be too far from the loo. A colostomy gives you your life back – you just have 'your bum on your tum' as colostomates say.

It's a shock at first but you are taught how to manage the bag. People worry that it will smell, or leak, but modern products are very efficient and discreet. No one will know unless you choose to tell them. In time you learn how your diet affects your bag and how often you need to change. There's nothing that we can't do – travel, go swimming, even run marathons if we want to.

Sometimes partners find it hard to deal with at first but most are supportive – all they want is you home, well again. Young people without partners wonder when they should tell a new boyfriend. You have to trust someone, and once they know you as a person it makes no difference.

I would always recommend contacting the Colostomy Association and talking to other people who really know how it feels.

11

Complementary medicine

Because digestive disorders are so common and so uncomfortable to live with, many patients turn to complementary therapies. Local pharmacists offer racks of different remedies for indigestion and your GP may prescribe the latest wonder drug, but conventional medicine does not seem to have all the answers. Many of the women I spoke to for this book had tried just about every over-the-counter and prescription medicine on offer and had found either that they didn't help, or that they caused side effects which were more troublesome than the original condition! Hence the popularity of so-called 'alternatives'.

If you are considering consulting a complementary practitioner for any health condition you need to remember

- that it's vital to make sure the person you consult is properly qualified, for example, that they belong to a professional organization such as the National Institute of Medical Herbalists (contact details on p. 116);
- that there are few scientific studies which prove that many complementary remedies actually work.

Having said that, some people do find them helpful. Professor Edzard Ernst, Britain's only Professor of Complementary Medicine, says there are no simple answers. 'There are so many different kinds of complementary therapies and so many different digestive problems. All we can say is that some of them seem to work for some conditions,' he says.

It is sometimes claimed that the apparent effectiveness of complementary treatments is just the result of the 'placebo effect' – this means that if you believe a treatment is going to do you good, then it probably will – but if it soothes your sore stomach or makes you feel less nauseous, why should you care? One of the main advantages of most complementary treatments is that consultations take much longer than the average appointment with a busy GP. This can be therapeutic in itself. We have already seen in Chapter 7 that many digestive problems are stress-related. It follows that any kind of therapy that you find relaxing, from a yoga class to a massage, may be beneficial. It is important, if you are already being treated for a digestive disorder, to tell your GP that you are thinking of consulting a complementary practitioner, too. Many GPs are much more open-minded about the value of 'alternatives' than they used to be.

The most common complementary therapies on offer in the UK today include herbal medicine, homoeopathy, acupuncture, traditional Chinese medicine and naturopathy. In the context of digestive disorders, nutrition therapy also deserves a mention. There are a lot of people out there who claim that changing your diet can cure all sorts of illnesses, including digestive disorders. Would you really feel better if you ate all-organic food, or raw food, or went on a diet of wheatgrass, seaweed and brown rice, or went in for a regular 'detox' or colonic irrigation? Could ginger, peppermint, mastic gum, silica gel, extract of artichoke, liquorice, aloe vera or Manuka honey really make a difference to your digestion? Many medical experts are sceptical ... but are they right? Let's look at some of the popular complementary therapies in more detail.

Herbal medicine

At one time, all medicines were 'herbal medicines'. Traditional herbalists, the 'wise women' of the past, had learned through centuries of experience that herbs could be used in the treatment of all sorts of ills from bruising to poisoning. They were right in many cases. Some modern drugs are derived from, or related to, the herbal lotions and potions of the past. Willow bark contains a substance similar to aspirin and morphine is derived from the opium poppy. Long-established companies like Potters have a range of herbal remedies which have been tried and tested over the years and include treatments for indigestion and heartburn, traveller's tummy, constipation and piles. They can be bought over the counter in pharmacies and health-food shops. For more detailed advice, you are advised to consult a qualified medical herbalist (see p. 116 for contact details).

Homoeopathy

Homoeopathy is one of the best-established complementary therapies. Treatment is sometimes available on the NHS at one of the five UK homoeopathic hospitals. Like many complementary therapies, homoeopathy concentrates on treating the whole person, not just the symptoms of ill-health, so a consultation with a homoeopathic doctor takes much longer than the ten minutes you get in the average GP consultation. A homoeopath will need to know all about the patient before prescribing a remedy tailored to the individual.

The basic principle of homoeopathy is that 'like cures like'. This means that any illness is treated with a substance which, in a healthy subject, produces the same symptoms displayed by the patient, the idea being to trigger the body's own healing processes. The founder of homoeopathy, Dr Samuel Hahnemann, found by experimenting that the more diluted the remedy, the more effective it was, and that extremely diluted remedies didn't produce unpleasant side effects. This is one reason why conventional scientists find it hard to believe that homoeopathic remedies can be effective, since some seem to contain such minute quantities of active ingredient. You can buy homoeopathic remedies over the counter in many pharmacies, but you need to choose the remedy most suited to your personality and temperament, as well as one recommended for your symptoms.

For example, if you have indigestion, you could try:

- *arsen. alb.* if you find digesting fruit, cold drinks and acidic foods difficult and if you also have diarrhoea;
- *bryonia* if indigestion comes on straight after you have eaten and you feel pain between the shoulderblades;
- *nux. vom.* if you have eaten too much, especially spicy foods, and your stomach feels heavy and swollen;
- *pulsatilla* if the pain comes on one or two hours after eating and you enjoy rich food, even though it makes the symptoms worse;
- *sulphur* if you're a long-term sufferer who has over-indulged in food and alcohol.

For a more detailed diagnosis, it's best to consult a qualified homoeopath.

Traditional Chinese medicine or TCM

Traditional Chinese medicine works on completely different principles from Western medicine and has been used to treat all forms of illness for around 5,000 years. Chinese doctors believe that good health depends on the correct flow of the life-force known as qi or chi throughout the body. This life-force is channelled along 12 pathways or 'meridians', six of them being Yin (feminine, cold, passive) and the other six being Yang (masculine, hot, active). The aim of traditional Chinese medicine is to balance these elements and ensure the smooth flow of qi to cure sickness and achieve good health.

Two of the most common treatments are acupuncture and Chinese herbs. Acupuncture is accepted by many Western doctors as well as Chinese physicians as a useful form of pain relief. It involves the insertion of very fine needles at appropriate points along the 'meridians'. Other forms of treatment are available for those who can't tolerate needles, although acupuncture is said not to be painful.

Chinese medicine is based on syndromes, not just symptoms, which means that a consultation with a Chinese physician will involve questions about your general health as well as your digestion. Your pulse will be taken and your tongue examined before any diagnosis is made and treatment suggested. It's especially important to make sure any Chinese practitioner you consult is properly qualified and that any herbal medicines prescribed are made from safe and effective ingredients.

Not all acupuncturists are experts in TCM; some are conventional health practitioners who have trained in this form of therapy. Members of the British Acupuncture Council (BAC) (contact details on p. 114) have all undergone a three-year training at an accredited college.

BAC member Jessica Kennedy practises in London and has found that acupuncture can help with many digestive conditions including heartburn, acid reflux and IBS.

'A condition like IBS is diagnosed differently in Chinese medicine,' she says.

> I give patients a lengthy questionnaire to fill in, and then an hour's consultation about all aspects of their health including whether they are hot or cold, whether they get headaches and how they deal with emotions. IBS symptoms could be the result of an imbalance in the spleen, the liver or elsewhere, which will probably encompass other, non-digestive symptoms too. All treatments are tailored to the individual and may include acupuncture, a herb called moxa, and also 'cupping' where cups are applied to different parts of the body. Some patients respond better than others.

Naturopathy

Naturopaths believe that the human body has the built-in ability to heal itself and that the cause of all disease is an accumulation of waste products and toxins as the result of unhealthy lifestyle. Treatments are directed at supporting this natural ability to heal and will include things like fresh air, whole foods, plenty of fresh water, healthy exercise, sunlight and relaxation. The belief is that symptoms like diarrhoea should not be suppressed with drugs as they are the body's natural way of ridding itself of toxins.

All treatments offered are completely natural and, depending on the condition being treated, may include advice on diet, hydrotherapy (including hot and cold baths), massage, counselling and relaxation techniques, the idea being to bring the body back into proper, balanced good health.

Some of the principles of naturopathy are controversial, including the disdain for drugs such as antibiotics and the advice not to vaccinate children against childhood diseases. However, much of the advice given – to avoid smoking and alcohol, too much tea and coffee and over-processed food – is now accepted wisdom and those with chronic digestive complaints such as persistent constipation or IBS may benefit from a consultation with a naturopath.

Nutritional therapy

Nutritional therapy is more than just advice on healthy eating. A therapist will work with a client to help the body rid itself of any food item which is causing problems, and to help in the absorption of food so that the patient benefits from the full range of required nutrients. It isn't so much that 'you are what you eat' as 'you are what your body can absorb'.

'Conventional medical students get very little training in nutrition,' says Suzanne Bryson of the London-based Institute for Optimum Nutrition (contact details on p. 115), which offers students a three-year training in nutritional therapy.

> We believe that many digestive conditions can be treated by dietary factors. When someone contacts one of our therapists we give them a four-page questionnaire on their diet and life-style and then a one-and-a-half-hour consultation, resulting in an individual, tailor-made programme for them, not just a diet sheet. We look at everything from their family history to other symptoms such as headaches, joint pains, lack of energy and stress levels.

Some people's digestive systems don't absorb nutrients properly. If your digestion doesn't work very well, it's simply less efficient at extracting the goodness from food and at eliminating the unwanted matter that is left behind. Anyone who has been treated with a lot of antibiotics can suffer from 'dysbiosis' – a build-up of 'bad' bacteria and yeasts in the gut which can lead to irritation of the digestive tract and general ill-health.

A good nutritional therapist will prescribe the correct diet for your individual problem and may also suggest you take a variety of supplements. The Sussex-based Natural Health Advisory Service/Women's Nutrition Clinic has been treating women for all kinds of health problems since 1987. Founder Maryon Stewart began by treating gynaecological symptoms such as pre-menstrual syndrome (PMS) and menopause difficulties by nutritional rather than chemical means. The Clinic's work soon broadened to include treatment for all women's health problems including digestive problems like constipation, indigestion, gastric reflux and IBS. It offers tailor-made advice and recommendations based on public medical research and years of clinical experience. Contact details on p. 115.

The truth about detox

We hear a lot about 'detox diets' these days and glossy magazines are full of stories of celebrities ascribing their good health and looks to expensive sessions with the latest strange diet or 'detox' kit.

The principle of a 'detox' isn't all bad. If you eat too much junk food, drink too much alcohol, start your day with a couple of double-strength espresso coffees and are 'too busy' to eat until the evening, by which time you are so starving that you overload your stomach with food and wine, it's no wonder that you have digestive problems. Taking it easy, cutting down on the nutritional nightmares and eating healthily for a change can only do you good. However, most conventional doctors, nutritionists and dietitians feel that the idea that you need a special 'kit' or a raft of pills to enable your body to get rid of so-called 'toxins' is just not true.

At the beginning of 2006, the campaigning group 'Sense about Science' said quite firmly that water, fresh air and sleep were the best forms of 'detox' and that supplements, diets and special drinks were a waste of time and money. The human body, they said, is perfectly capable of ridding itself of harmful substances on its own. The gut actually prevents bacteria and other toxins from entering the body. The liver breaks down any harmful chemicals, which are then excreted by the kidneys.

In other words there is no scientific evidence that our bodies need help in getting rid of 'toxins', whether these are the result of environmental pollution, cigarette smoke, pesticides, junk food, additives, alcohol or caffeine. Nor is there any real proof that detox diets work. They do vary, and a diet rich in fresh fruit and vegetables, nuts and seeds with plenty of water or herbal infusions to drink, is preferable to one loaded with high-fat, high-sugar processed foods.

However, any detox diet which suggests you give up staple foods like wheat, dairy, meat or fish on a long-term basis needs to be carefully worked out by a qualified dietitian, or you risk nutritional deficiencies. Vegetarians, who eat no meat or fish, vegans, who eat no animal products at all, and coeliacs, who can't tolerate gluten, can all have perfectly healthy diets, but they do need to be carefully balanced. Vegetarians and vegans may need supplements of vitamin B12 or iron, anyone avoiding dairy products runs the risk of calcium deficiency leading to brittle bones or osteoporosis, and coeliacs need to find substitutes for the wheat-based products they can't tolerate.

As well as a limited diet, a detox may also involve treatments like saunas and massage, which can be very relaxing, enemas and 'colonic irrigation', otherwise known as colonic hydrotherapy, in which warm water is passed into the rectum and through the bowel to 'flush out' faecal remains and any 'bad' bacteria.

There doesn't seem to be any real medical evidence that a 'colonic' is effective, but some people find it can help with chronic conditions like wind, bloating, constipation or IBS. A treatment will last about 40 minutes and the therapist massages the abdomen at the same time to help in the 'flushing' process. As a colonic tends to get rid of friendly as well as bad bacteria, you may be given probiotics afterwards to repopulate your gut with the right kind of bacteria.

What about supplements?

If you go into your local health-food store you will be overwhelmed with the number of pills, potions and miracle ingredients which promise you better digestive health. Holland & Barrett stores, for example, have 41 different products for digestive conditions and their staff are trained to give advice on the most suitable for your particular circumstances. If you find that the range of products from the pharmacy or the pills your doctor has prescribed seem to have little effect, it's always tempting to try an 'alternative' and see if it works for you. Unfortunately, there are few scientific studies to prove one way or the other that these products do any good. Some of them do seem to help some people and they aren't likely to do any harm.

Some everyday products are worth considering. Peppermint tea, for instance, can be soothing for a sore stomach and can help the digestion if you drink it after a meal instead of coffee. Peppermint, along with caraway and fennel, is known as a 'carminative' herb which means that it can ease griping pains and help with flatulence. Ginger has been proven effective in treating nausea. Honey is another store-cupboard item which has been extensively studied as a digestive aid.

Honey has been known for its anti-bacterial, healing properties for thousands of years. It was used by the Ancient Greeks, Egyptians and Indians to keep wounds free of infection. In recent years Professor Peter Molan of Waikato University in New Zealand has been studying active Manuka honey, which seems to be especially effective in destroying harmful bacteria, including the *H. pylori* bacterium which is now known to cause stomach ulcers.

'Our research is ongoing, and we have more to learn, but the patients we have worked with who had ulcers or gastritis felt more comfortable after being treated with Manuka honey,' he says.

> This kind of honey seems particularly effective against *H. pylori*. Other types of honey have an anti-inflammatory effect and may help with any inflammatory gut disorder. As far as I know there is no research to prove honey helps conditions like IBS, ulcerative colitis or Crohn's, but I am often contacted by people with these conditions who have found it effective. It is not scientific, but it's encouraging.

Professor Molan recommends a heaped spoonful of active Manuka honey before meals if you have a sore stomach or an ulcer.

Aloe vera is another natural product which has been used for its medicinal properties for many thousands of years. The plant is a succulent, related to lilies, onions, garlic and asparagus. It is known to contain at least 75 ingredients which can benefit health and well-being, including vitamins, minerals, amino acids, enzymes and plant sterols. Former GP Dr Peter Atherton has studied the properties of aloe vera for years and says, 'It isn't myth or magic, it's medicine. Drinking aloe vera gel can provide the body with micronutrients missing from our modern diets.'

Dr Atherton has treated IBS patients with aloe vera gel and says that about half found it beneficial. It has a powerful anti-inflammatory action and can therefore help in the treatment of inflammatory bowel diseases such as ulcerative colitis and Crohn's, as shown by a clinical trial at the Royal London Hospital.

Many of the products you'll find in health-food stores are based on traditional remedies for digestive problems. For example, mastic gum, a resin produced by an evergreen shrub related to the pistachio family, has been used for 300 years in the Middle East to treat gastric problems. Researchers at Nottingham University in the 1990s found that it was effective against the *H. pylori* bacterium implicated in the development of ulcers. Liquorice is used in traditional Chinese medicine to boost liver function and is also a traditional remedy for gastritis, ulcers and colic. Artichoke extract, recommended by Classic FM radio doctor Rob Hicks, helped 70 per cent of those suffering from symptoms like indigestion, IBS, nausea and constipation in a clinical trial. Milk thistle is another traditional remedy for digestive disorders.

Useful addresses

There are many organizations, pressure groups and helplines for those who have digestive disorders, and an equal number aimed at helping with the habits – such as smoking, drinking and stress – which can make digestive problems worse.

AcuMedic Chinese Medical Centre
101–105 Camden High Street
London NW1 7JN
Tel.: 020 7388 6704
Website: www.acumedic.com

Acupuncturist Jessica Kennedy
Tel.: 020 7928 7705
Website: www.jessicakennedy.com

Alcoholics Anonymous
PO Box 1
10 Toft Green
York YO1 7NJ
Tel.: 0845 769 7555
Website: www.alcoholics-anonymous.org.uk

Allergy UK
3 White Oak Square
London Road
Swanley
Kent BR8 7AG
Tel.: 01322 619898
Website: www.allergyuk.org

Bowel Cancer UK
7 Rickett Street
London SW6 1RU
Tel.: 0800 8 40 35 40
Website: www.bowelcanceruk.org.uk

British Acupuncture Council
63 Jeddo Road
London W12 9HQ
Tel.: 020 8735 0400
Website: www.acupuncture.org.uk

British Autogenic Society
c/o Royal London Homoeopathic
Hospital
60 Great Ormond Street
London WC1N 3HR
Tel.: 020 7391 8908
Website: www.autogenic-therapy.org.uk

British Homoeopathic Association
Hahnemann House
29 Park Street West
Luton LU1 3BE
Tel.: 0870 444 3950
Website: www.trusthomeopathy.org

British Nutrition Foundation
High Holborn House
52–54 High Holborn
London WC1V 6RQ
Tel.: 020 7404 6504
Website: www.nutrition.org.uk

British Wheel of Yoga
25 Jermyn Street
Sleaford
Lincs. NG34 7RU
Tel.: 01529 306851
Website: www.bwy.org.uk

Cancerbackup
3 Bath Place
Rivington Street
London EC2A 3JR
Helpline: 0808 800 1234
Website: www.cancerbackup.org.uk

Cancer Research UK
PO Box 123
Lincoln's Inn Fields
London WC2A 3PX
Tel.: 020 7242 0200
Website: www.cancerresearchuk.org

Coeliac UK
Suites A–D, Octagon Court
High Wycombe
Bucks HP11 2HS
Helpline: 0870 444 8804
Website: www.coeliac.org.uk

Colostomy Association
15 Station Road
Reading RG1 1LG
Helpline: 0800 328 4257 or 0800 587 6744
Website: www.colostomyassociation. org.uk

Complementary Healthcare Information Service
Website: www.chisuk.org.uk

CORE (the Digestive Disorders Foundation)
3 St Andrews Place
London NW1 4LB
Website: www.corecharity.org.uk

If writing for any of their factsheets, please enclose s.a.e.

Dietitian Emma Mills
Tel.: 01623 882853
Website: www.brainandbody.co.uk

Foods Matter
5 Lawn Road
London NW3 2XS
Tel.: 020 7722 2866
Website: www.foodsmatter.com

Gaiam Ltd
Northfield Road
Southam
Warwickshire CV47 0RD
Tel.: 0870 241 5471
Website: www.gaiamdirect.co.uk

Producer of a range of fitness and relaxation products including DVDs.

The Gut Trust (formerly the IBS Network)
Unit 5, 53 Mowbray Street
Sheffield S3 8EN
Tel.: 0114 272 3253
Website: www.theguttrust.org

Institute for Optimum Nutrition
Avalon House
72 Lower Mortlake Road
Richmond
Surrey TW9 2JY
Tel.: 0870 979 1122
Website: www.ion.ac.uk

National Association for Colitis and Crohn's Disease
4 Beaumont House
Sutton Road
St Albans
Herts AL1 5HH
Information Line: 0845 130 2233
Website: www.nacc.org.uk

Natural Health Advisory Service (formerly the Women's Nutritional Advisory Service)
PO Box 117
Rottingdean
Brighton
East Sussex BN51 9BG
Tel.: 01273 609699
Website: www.naturalhealthas.com

National Institute of Medical Herbalists
Elm House
54 Mary Arches Street
Exeter EX4 3BA
Tel.: 01392 426022
Website: www.nimh.org.uk

NHS Stop Smoking
Helpline: 0800 169 0169
Website: http://gosmokefree.nhs.uk/

QUIT
Helpline: 0800 002200
Website: www.quit.org.uk

Relate
Central Office
Tel.: 0300 100 1234
Website: www.relate.org.uk

T'ai Chi Union for Great Britain
Tel.: 01403 257918
Website: www.taichiunion.com

Vegan Society
Donald Watson House
21 Hylton Street
Hockley
Birmingham B18 6HJ
Tel.: 0845 458 8244
Website: www.vegansociety.com

Vegetarian Society of the UK
Parkdale
Dunham Road
Altrincham
Cheshire WA14 4QG
Tel.: 0161 925 2000
Website: www.vegsoc.org

YorkTest Laboratories Ltd
York Science Park
York YO10 5DQ
Tel.: 0800 458 2052
Website: www.yorktest.com

Provide finger-prick bloodtesting services to assess food intolerances and other allergies.

Index

117